T0065366

THE DILEMMA OF THE BLACKMAN

Enhancing the African's Dignity

SORIE I KAMARA

authorHOUSE®

AuthorHouse™
1663 Liberty Drive
Bloomington, IN 47403
www.authorhouse.com
Phone: 833-262-8899

*This is a work of fiction. All of the characters, names, incidents,
organizations, and dialogue in this novel are either the products
of the author's imagination or are used fictitiously.*

Published by AuthorHouse 01/22/2021

ISBN: 978-1-6655-1486-6 (sc)
ISBN: 978-1-6655-1493-4 (e)

Print information available on the last page.

This book is printed on acid-free paper.

To my grandchildren and great-grandchildren and to Black people and those yet unborn. I hope they will realize that what they see glittering before them is not all gold. Their ancestors were killed and subjected to the most inhuman treatment the human being can exert on a fellow human. Religion is good for spiritual satisfaction. But which religion?

As a people, we have lost the full sense of our being,
we hang in a limbo of cultural confusion, social incoherence,
political chaos, economic despair and moral purposelessness.
We have, in this condition, come to believe
500 years of European propaganda
and brainwashing, that we are inferior to the
European and his ways, his thought
system, his material civilization, his skin color,
and that his God is superior to ours.

by an act of retrievance and reconnection, the true history,
The culture of Africa, our religious institutions and philosophic
Notions of man and the world must be
recovered, properly researched and
written down.

—Professor Kofi Awoonor

CONTENTS

PREFACE

> As more and more Africans become disillusioned with
> the lack of political, social, and economic gains from the
> modern state, loyalty to the tribal order is spreading.
> —BBC African Perspective, *Children of the Drum*

Fellow Blackman,

Since this program was first aired on the BBC African Service, and the advent of social media, a lot has happened vis-à-vis Black issues and problems. Among these are the continuous random killing of young Blacks in the United States and the wretched treatment they receive in Western Europe.

For me, the most important event in history is the diminishing role, power, or influence of Britain in world affairs, as Britannia no longer rules the oceans and the increasing awareness of the problems black people still face at the hands of white people.

Walter McRae, a Black West Indian theologian, describes a Blackman as somebody who is

- Black in color,
- Black in Negroid characteristics [black curly hair, flat wide nose, thick lips, dark brown eyes, and prominent heels][1]
- Black in black ancestry
- [and black in thought].[2]

---

[1] The characteristics are my understanding, as Walter McRae never explained them.

[2] This is my addition, for children of Black fathers and White mothers and vice versa who are brought up Black, think Black, and do everything Black cannot be deprived of their Blackness if they claim it.

Religion is a way people feel they can worship what they believe in—God Almighty or a Supreme Being or the Ultimate, be it Christianity, Judaism, Islam, Buddhism, Hinduism, or Shintoism. Religion carries many different meanings to many different people.

All these religions could be related to certain population groups—for example, Christianity to Europeans and people of European descent, Judaism specifically to the Jews, Islam to the Arabs and Arab-related people, Hinduism to the Hindi-speaking people of India, Buddhism to China and Chinese-related people of Asia, and finally Shintoism specifically to the Japanese.

It is also a clear fact that these religions are expressed with the cultures of the peoples they are identified with, as no definite line could be drawn between their respective cultures and their religions.

What about the Blackman or African? What religion identifies him?

If you are deeply religious, I will urge you to separate *religion* (the way you feel you can worship what you believe in) and *faith* (the belief you have in the way you worship).

If you overlap the two, then you will totally misread the message, and your reaction will be hostile. But if you can separate the two, then the message will come home, awakening you.

You may not have looked at the issues as presented. I have presented the issues this way for you to reflect on yourself, your people, and the Black diaspora. Some of the issues may offend and even annoy you, as you may have undergone a great psychological metamorphosis since childhood. But one thing that has not and will never change is your Blackness, and I want that Blackness to act as a restraining force on you.

I wish you a pleasant reading.

CHAPTER 1

Early Religious Beliefs

Anthropology, or rather social anthropology, has finally settled on the belief that humans, as *Homo sapiens*, first appeared in that part of Africa where the Rift Valley is.

As the population increased, so did groups, societies, and communities. Curiosity set in as to how or why they were there and who or what was responsible. Who created the environment they were living in and the forces that let them be who they were? They became curious about everything that concerned their lives.

Early Africans believed that there was a supernatural being overseeing all their activities—hunting, feeding, shelter, farming, and all aspects of daily life.

As their numbers increased, what has been described as the "mass migration" started, when Africans started to explore that vast continent called Africa.

As the migration expanded, so too did their beliefs in *the* Supernatural Being—that he was directing their lives and their every move in ways they could not understand, as he could not be seen. The fact that he could not be seen created a serious problem, as they could only attempt to talk to him, rather than see him. That confusion, in my opinion, led them to devise the many ways of communicating with him, which have resulted also in the many different names, all meaning the same.

In Africa, there are many names for the Supernatural Being, as each tribe has its own. The environment or locality played a huge role in their everyday lives—most importantly, how to satisfy the unseen power.

Farming was especially important in the lives of early Africans, and since the yields depended on the unpredictable weather, something had to be done to satisfy that Supernatural Being; hence, prayer and worshipping took shape. This was the early sign of religion, if religion can be understood to be one's connection to his or her Creator.

Irrespective of where the Africans migrated on the continent, one common thread of belief permeated—that there was a Supernatural Being who was all-powerful but whom they could not see but could talk to. This confusion was fueled by the environment they happened to find themselves in and the forces influencing them.

One grave and, I daresay, deliberately wicked mistake by Europeans at the time was their refusal even to try to understand the psyche of the African people they met. They approached the Africans from a presumption of superiority, like that expressed by Sir Samuel Baker in his address to the Ethnological Society in London in 1866: "Without any exception they are without a belief in a Supreme Being. Neither have they any form of worship nor idolatry nor is the darkness of their minds enlightened by even a ray of superstition. The mind is as stagnant as the morass which forms its puny world."

Nothing could be more misleading—Baker's words simply demonstrate his ignorance of anthropology at the time. But during those times, the British Empire dominated the world, and anything said by them was unchallenged.

From what I have described, it should be abundantly clear that religion, or the belief in God or a Supernatural Being, has always been fundamental in the daily lives of Africans, then and now. Any attempt to separate the African from his or her belief in the Supernatural Being and the environment is totally missing the point, but Europeans constantly do that to satisfy themselves and their gullible populations about their superiority over Black people.

Religion or the belief in a Supernatural Being is in the everyday life of the Black African, as expressed in the different names given to God among the many different tribes in Africa. Each tribe or ethnic group— the Hausa, the Yoruba, the Wolof, the Susu, the Mandingo, the Igbo, the

Swahili, the Zulu, and the Xhosa, to name a few—has its own name for God that is separate and different from the others.

In *An Introduction to the Study of African Culture* (third edition), E. O. Ayisi commented:

> Sociologists and social anthropologists have treated African religion as if it were a bizarre museum item entirely different from other religious phenomena found in western culture. They have given it a conceptual interpretation that betrays their prejudices about African cultures, which in many ways, are not valid and lack rational justification. There has been too much confused thinking about the religious practices and beliefs of Africans. Africans have been described by some writers as pagans, heathens, or men whose lives are dominated and trammeled by superstitions. It has been said that they lack any theological ideas and that all the elements, which make Judaism, Islam, or Christianity sublime, are lacking in African religion. People who should have known better, especially missionaries, were completely misguided about African religion, and by their muddled thinking propagated erroneous ideas about African religious beliefs.

Before Africans got their independence from Europe, history, or rather everything, about Africans was written by Europeans or the Whiteman. This trend is true for the history of Black people in the United States, but as more and more Black people have become educated, fewer White people in the United States and internationally now claim authority on the history of Black people. This change aligns with the vision of Professor Kofi Awoonor, as expressed in one of his numerous lectures, "Enhancing the African's Dignity":

So, it is so refreshing to see and read the numerous research papers and books written by Africans themselves about history created by those very Africans and for Africans, which no Whiteman dares anymore to distort. How the world has changed!

African people's belief in God was not brought to them through Christianity or Islam. That belief developed from within them and was passed on from generation to generation, as with other peoples of the world. That tradition is fundamental and deep in the psyche of the African, so much so that those who accept Christianity or Islam simply blend their beliefs with their newfound ones—with an ease that Europeans and Arabs can hardly comprehend.

Since the advent of colonialism, traditional African beliefs have been under constant and relentless pressure from what the late Professor Arthur Abraham of Virginia University described to me as the concept of "tabula rasa" (blank slate). This means that, for one to be a Christian, everything must change except one's skin color, thereby enticing one to privileged situations as a benefit for being a Christian; as a result, one's African beliefs are treated as fossil beliefs. Like all other aspects of human development, traditional African beliefs cannot stay steadfast and untouched forever, but at the same time they cannot be rendered irrelevant as a historic relic in the way that born-again Christians are doing.

Europeans through the centuries have used every derogatory term available to demean traditional African beliefs—for example, *juju*, *fetish*, *heathen*, and *pagan*. Evangelical Christianity in the United States these days comes with an air of superiority over traditional African beliefs, taking advantage of the poverty endemic to the continent. They go into deep villages where poverty is the order of the day and provide food, shelter, medicines, and other goods—all that the local governments could not give them. Unsuspecting, the people are bought, and who can blame them?

Africans believe in their traditions, the beliefs that constitute their raison d'être, and have effortlessly blended their beliefs with new ones, from especially the United States—born-again Christianity.

Africans' Beliefs in Different Aspects of Life

For the African, life and death are a continuous process, as one transforms into another. There must be life before death, and death is a continuation of life but in a different form. Many tribes in Africa would prefer not to have an autopsy conducted if it can be avoided. The Ashanti, I am told, would always prefer to avoid autopsy to allow the body to go whole into the world beyond to continue life.

From all that I have written, it should now be clear that the Blackman was the first to appear as *Homo sapiens* on this earth. Consequently, the Blackman had his own interpretation or understanding of the universe—that is, the world around him. In my research, Professor Ali Mazrui's remarks in his BBC series *Africans, the Triple Heritage* stand out:

> In traditional African beliefs, the forces of creation and the things created are part of the same reality, but Christianity and Islam brought a God who was or is separate from the creative, enthroned in heaven while man has been made king over the animals below, the natural world was thus made a servant of man rather than a partner.
>
> African religion believes that it was not just man who was created in the image of God, the whole universe has been created thus, in fact the universe and the creative process are a kind of autobiography of God, God narrating his story chapter by chapter, tree by tree, star by star, stream by stream, and all the different elements in nature are expressions of God—the sunrise—God's smile, the drought—the wrath of the ancestors so that is why each time there is drought or poor harvest black Africans invoke the spirits of their ancestors by offering sacrifices which both religions condemn; lightening is interpreted as a divine orgasm.

One concept of death among some Africans, such as the Kissi in Sierra Leone, is reincarnation, the rebirth of a soul in another person. If or when a woman continues to be losing children after birth, there comes a time when a decision is made to mark the child that is immediately lost, at times with a wooden splinter pushed under the nail of any finger or a scarification made on the upper inner thigh. This is all done to see if it is the same child that is being repeatedly born. In some or most cases, it is the same child.

The bedrock of the African's belief is ancestral worship. The ancestors are the people who lived on that land before them and have died and transformed to spirits that can see that whom they cannot, the Creator, God Almighty. The ancestors know them well and can transmit their problems better than they can. For that to happen, the ancestors must be pleased in many different and diverse ways—ceremonies, sacrifices, rituals, and the like. Libations are poured to satisfy the ancestors. At funerals, lots of oral messages are sent through the dead to the ancestors to protect the families the deceased came from, gain prosperity for that family, and so on. The methods used to revere the ancestors vary from society to society, locality to locality, and tribe to tribe. When, in 1993, the then young military leader of Sierra Leone Brigadier Bio, incidentally the present civilian President, visited President Jerry Rawlings of Ghana, he was met at Kotoka International airport by Rawlings and a traditional priest, not a Christian pastor or an Islamic cleric, thereby emphasizing the important role the ancestors play in African relations. Ghanaians, whom I met and asked, told me that the traditional priest was to invoke the spirits of the ancestors, to check whether the visitor or stranger meant good or bad and to take care of his visit to protect the community. That was remarkably like what happens in most, if not all, of Black Africa.

Africans have no prophets, as their belief in the Creator comes directly from their belief in his omnipresence and omnipotence. Since they cannot see or feel their Creator, it is only left to their imagination, which is interpreted in reverence for their deities. These can be represented in different forms, by mostly statuettes—criticized by Europeans and converted Africans as represented in this Congolese song of the 1960s titled "Nakomitunaka":

"Nakomitunaka"

I ask myself; God I ask myself,

Yaweh, I ask myself,

Where did black skin come from?

Who are our ancestors?

Jesus, the Son of God is white, Adam and Eve are white, all the saints are white. Why is that? ...

In the Holy Books of God, we see images of all Saints as white people, all angels are depicted as white. If it is a demon, it is depicted as a black person. (Orchestre Veve)

This Congolese song by Orchestre Veve, with Kia Muangana sung just after independence to remind Africans how Europeans had manipulated them into believing in the religion of the Europeans and forgetting that of their ancestors.

All over Africa where chieftaincy exists, when a chief is crowned or installed, the language used is not that of strangers from distant lands but, rather, language and rituals as laid down by their ancestors as guardians of the land where they exist. This is passed on from generation to generation, as in Sierra Leone, where I hail from, the Ashanti, the Zulu, the Xhosa, and many others.

CHAPTER 2

Marriage

M arriage was and still is an especially important aspect of African communal life, as it is considered the bringing together of two or more families through one man and one woman or one man and more than one woman. It is considered, as indeed in all other societies in the world, as the last stage of a young individual's maturity and beginning of responsibility.

The criteria used to determine when a young individual should marry vary from society to society, clan to clan, and tribe to tribe. In some tribes, the passage to maturity for boys is determined after circumcision, mostly after age sixteen. But some of the methods of circumcision were so brutal that the criteria had to change. With modernity, the age has been reduced to just after birth, and circumcision is done by specialized medical people. The criterion then to marry, for the male, started changing from the parents looking out for a suitable bride to allowing the young male to choose for himself.

For the girls, when the breast increases in size to being at right angles to the chest, then she is ready to be given out in marriage. For others, the determination is made as soon as her menstruation starts, others for many different reasons, finances being the most compelling. his has provoked serious criticisms about childhood marriage.

The girl child is prepared for marital life. In some countries, in West Africa, like Sierra Leone there are secret female societies, the Bondo, where female circumcision is practiced and the participants are taught how to care for their future husbands, their households, and their children. Most important for the individual families is whether the girl is chaste. If she is not, then that brings a lot of shame to the respective family, with pecuniary fines. With evolution and modernity, all those aspects have come under severe criticism and pressure and are gradually losing their importance. There are about 24 countries in Africa that have banned the practice of female circumcision.

As in Europe, where rich people always go after their kind and peasants after theirs to marry, in Africa, marriage being a particularly important part of life, mothers of the husbands to be, for fear of losing their grip on their sons, always seek the help of clairvoyants or astrologers to know whether a prospective bride would be a good wife for their sons. When we were taught British and European history, one thing that came to light was how marriages were used to acquire and expand kingdoms.

Another aspect of marriage in traditional Africa is polygamy. This came under severe criticism from the White Christian missionaries, who applied the tabula rasa concept to their African converts, forcing them to agree to cleanse themselves of every vestige of their cultural heritage except their skin color. Their names were changed to Christian names. They could not attend any traditional shows. They had to let go every practice outside of Christianity that had once made up their worlds. In Kenya as indeed most if not all the British colonies, Africans learned quickly how to accommodate the new system. They would marry one woman in full view of the church, while getting a second by traditional rites in their villages of birth.

But why was polygamy necessary at the time? Early Africans, as indeed early peoples the world over, were engaged in agriculture, as industrialization was not known then, and many hands were needed on the farm. The easiest way to do that was to marry more than one woman and have as many children as possible, which eased work on the farm. The Whiteman refused to understand that and continued denigrating Black Africans, as history has shown.

The other reason, some say, is male machismo, using plurality of wives as a prestige.

Still another reason for polygamy, as shown in the Quran and after World War II, is to reduce society's ills that are aggravated when many women remain unmarried. There are Christians of the Church of Jesus Christ of Latter-Day Saints—the Mormons—who practice polygamy. In Ghana, and indeed a few other African countries, Christian pastors have started advocating for polygamy to save society. The explanation can be understood through the many internecine wars that have been fought on the African continent, with mainly young men being sent to fight. This phenomenon is not exclusive to Africa. Most of the wars in history have been fought using young men. Every loss on the battlefield has been mainly of men, leaving the women without their partners. This has been glaring after the two world wars and all the wars that have engulfed the world's attention. There has been talk of a permissive society in the West that gave rise to the baby boomer generation.

Now that Africans have been studying European history deeply and widely, they can convince themselves that, apart from industrial and technological development, they have in no way been inferior to Europeans in human-to-human behavior. Black people have witnessed fear in the eyes of their colonial masters during the two world wars, have been able to save them from death in many cases, and have seen them scared to death. All this humanized the Whiteman as an ordinary human rather than the "superior beings" they portrayed themselves to be. World War II made Africans see the brutality White men exerted on their fellow Whites, not to mention non-Whites.

During the previous three centuries, the European or Whiteman had been crisscrossing the globe, meeting different population groups, decimating some, and subduing others, spreading disease in the process. They mingled with these groups, traded with them, and studied them—only to come back and misinterpret and denigrate those societies to their own people to make them feel superior. This is a feeling that, unfortunately, has continued to this date.

As I said earlier, Sir Samuel Baker wrote in 1866 of the people of the Northern Nilotes, "Without any exception they are without a belief in a Supreme Being. Neither have they any form of worship nor idolatry nor is the darkness of their minds enlightened by even a ray of superstition. The mind is as stagnant as the morass which forms its puny world." This was dishonest on his part, as in 1870, Bishop Tozier of Central African also said rightly, "What do we mean when we say that England

and France are civilized countries and that the greater part of Africa is uncivilized? Surely, the mere enjoyment of such things as railways and telegraphs do not necessarily prove their possessors in the first rank of civilization. Nothing can be so false as to suppose that the outward circumstances of a people are the measure of its barbarism or its civilization."

It is clear how these early explorers arrogated to themselves the right to speak about Africans as they deemed fit, misleading, and misguiding their own people about Black Africans. King Leopold II of Belgium, having been now convinced that Black Africans know God, sent this message to his missionaries going to the Congo: "Your principal objective in our mission to the Congo, is never to teach the niggers to know God, this they know already." They had to concentrate on getting the people to obey them.

CHAPTER 3

The Transatlantic Slave Trade

I n 1979, Professor Ali Mazrui, in one of his Reith lectures, said that slavery not only dehumanized the Black African but, most importantly, also devalued him. The world has seen through documentaries on World War II how the Jews were severely dehumanized through the Holocaust during the Third Reich that ended with the end of the war in July 1945. The sale of Black Africans with its concomitant brutality lasted for centuries.

What provoked the slave trade? Some of us have discovered that, throughout history, greed was the basic motivator for the slave trade, as powerful nations at the time, like Portugal and Spain, saw the possibility to increase their power and influence by exploring distant lands for their underground riches, like gold, diamond and other minerals. Under pressure from these powers, the Roman Catholic Church divided the world arbitrarily into two halves, with Portugal having a monopoly on trade in West Africa while Spain took over in the New World of the Americas. Pope Nicholas V, in a bid to curry favor with them, wrote out the *Romanus Pontifex* in 1455, confirming Portugal's exclusive right to trade with territories it claimed in the West Coast of Africa and surrounding areas. The document also granted Portugal the right to invade, plunder, and "reduce their persons to perpetual slavery."

On the contrary, Queen Isabella of Spain rejected the enslavement of Native Americans, as she considered them Spanish subjects but invested in the activities of Christopher Columbus to increase her wealth. Spain gave out contract authorizing the direct shipment of captive Africans for trade as human commodities in Spanish colonies in the Americas. The floodgates were, thus, opened for other European powers—France, Belgium, Britain, Netherlands, and Denmark.

Before the scramble for Africa started, Europeans approached the indigenous people of Africa through what I can safely call the unholy trinity of religion, commerce, and politics. In many of the cases, missionaries went first, to soften the people to accepting the Whiteman, followed by explorers and then plunderers.

Through all these contacts, the hospitality of the people was exploited, and their weaknesses revealed. Through collaborators, Africans were caught and sold to White people, who later took their human cargo to unknown lands and sold them as slaves. I think, for the Africans of those years, a slave was somebody caught in intertribal or internecine wars and commanded to work as unpaid labor. In my opinion, the whole concept changed when foreigners came in with exchange for goods.

Slave ports sprung up everywhere along the west coast of Africa as the trade became popular and expanding – from Nigeria to Senegal. Africans of all ages and gender were captured and sold.

Once on board the slave ships, the slaves were packed in like sardines, and those who rebelled were severely whipped into submission. Imagine the psychological trauma suffered by a person who was used to roaming free in the bushes and plains in his or her area of birth upon suddenly being captured, taken on board a boat, and being whipped by people he or she had never seen before. Toilet facilities, one can only imagine, were horrible. How they must have been relieving themselves is unspeakable. No records exist on hygiene facilities on board slave ships, except as seen in Hollywood depictions. No treatment facilities were available; illnesses were always overlooked. The slaves were not seen as human but, rather, as cargo, so illness meant the slave was thrown overboard into the unforgiving ocean. This was how many slaves never reached their eventual destinations, instead swallowed up in the Atlantic Ocean, the Middle Passage. They were barely fed, and only the strong and perseverant survived the journey. Some estimates stated that up to 40 percent of enslaved people could not make it to their intended destinations in the Americas.

The 1619 Project, unveiled in *The New York Times* August 20th, 2019, has made it known to the world that, as early as August 1619, the colonists bought twenty to thirty enslaved Africans of both genders from Portuguese slave ships that had initially captured them from now Angola. This was the beginning of a slave trade that Jamestown brought 12.5 million Africans—kidnapped and brought over in chains in what is described as the largest forced migration in human history.

Once on American soil, the slaves were subjected to a brutality that humankind had never seen hitherto. This was captured in the song "Buffalo Soldier" by the late reggae artist Bob Marley, who sang about them "fighting on arrival, fighting for survival." They were not recognized as human beings but thought of and treated as property that could be mortgaged, traded, bought, sold, used as collateral, given as a gift, and disposed of violently. Their slavers were Christians who had run away from religious prosecution in England, but had put the teachings of Jesus Christ aside, preferring profit. Instead, they created a set of laws and practices to make sure the slaves were never treated as human beings.

The slaves were never to marry and prevented from learning and reading. They were prohibited from meeting in groups. A slave woman had no claim over the child she brought forth into this world, as the child could be bought, sold, and traded away without any regard for her feelings, on auction like furniture and cattle, thereby devaluing the Blackman. Slave markets erupted all over America, especially in slaveholding states, where advertisements like "Negroes for Sale" could be seen. Putting a human being in an open market for sale not only dehumanizes him but also devalues him. Let us not forget that the initial permission was given by the Pope, despite what the Bible said and still says.

The slaves were treated worse than dogs, as dogs were protected, fed, and given particularly good treatment. The slaves were not protected by law; they could be brutalized without recourse or legal protection.

Owners or masters could rape the slave women, even though they were not considered human, get them pregnant, and then take their children away from them and sell them off. They were legally tortured and even murdered at will. The slaves had no right to own or inherit property. Where was religion to protect these children of God as had been preached for centuries? Was religion only for White people? If not, why did the Pope give the okay for slavery to start, with all its concomitant brutality? I consider it hypocritical for the Catholic Church to turn around and make as if there was no evidence of such brutality.

The indiscriminate capture of Black Africans taken into slavery led to the kidnapping of Omar Ibn Said. He was captured in today's Senegal at age thirty-seven and brought to South Carolina, where he was bought. According to his own writing, his slave master was cruel to him. His story was part of a pattern of cruelty exerted on the slaves. This led to slaves beginning to revolt against their masters, thereby causing them great revenue losses. During the period in review, slaves had revolted many times against their captors at sea, at times killing their transporters. There are stories of empty slave ships landing on the shores of England with dead sailors. This revolt or rebellion continued even when they landed in the Americas. The most remarkable of such incidents was the story of Shengbe Pieh, a slave captured in Sierra Leone who was to be taken to the United States. He led his fellow captives to revolt. He and his companions were later arrested, taken to the United States, put on trial, judged, and freed.

In mainland America, the cruelty exerted on slaves was so unbearable that the slaves began to escape or revolt.

For those who escaped, their stories became legendary. In history, some of their stories became worthy of narration: Henry "Box" Brown, who escaped in a box after his wife and children were sold away to another state in 1848. During the journey, while in the box, the box was turned upside down on the deck of the steamship thereby sitting on his head with his eyes swelling and bulging out of his sockets. He nearly passed out but for two unsuspecting passengers who flipped the box to use as a seat. He was saved and arrived safely in Philadelphia. He had to flee to Great Britain after the passing of the Fugitive Slave Act. In

Britain he worked as a magician climbing to the same box that he fled in as part of his performance.

Frederick Douglas, who in 1838, fled Baltimore on board a train North. He was disguised in a sailor's uniform, provided by his future wife, Anna Murray. He had a free sailor's protection pass loaned to him by an accomplice. Frederick bore no resemblance to the man listed in the document and was apprehensive about what the conductor would do. Luckily for him, the conductor gave a cursory glance to the document before moving on to the next passenger. He later arrived in New York where he joined Murray and they both moved on to New Bedford, Massachusetts, where Douglas established himself as one of the nation's leading abolitionists.

There are many other like stories but the ones that shook the foundation of slave ownership was the violent revolt of slaves that cost not only loss of revenue by the lives of the slave owners themselves.

Among the revolts, there are three that stand out: Gabriel Prosser in Virginia in 1800, Denmark Vesey in Charleston, South Carolina in 1822, and the most famous and unforgettable, Nat Turner, in Southampton County, Virginia 1831.

The story of Nat Turner's rebellion provoked a lot of debates, disagreements, and misinterpretations by white people about blacks till present day America.

Who was Nat Turner? He was an African American, enslaved preacher, born on October 2, 1800. He led a rebellion of enslaved and free black people in Southampton County, Virginia, where there were more blacks than whites. He learned how to read and write at an early age and was described as having "natural intelligence and quickness of apprehension, surpassed by few". He was deeply religious and was often conducting services, preaching the Bible to his fellow enslaved people, who called him the "The Prophet". He also had white admirers like Etheldred T. Brantley, whom Turner was credited with having convinced to "cease from his wickedness".

Turner drew inspiration from the Bible and strongly believed that he "was ordained for some great purpose in the hands of the Almighty". He was very attracted to the actions of Jesus Christ in trying to free his people from domination and that "Christ had laid down the yoke he had borne for the sins of men, and that I should take it on and fight against the Serpent, for the time was fast approaching when the first should be last and the last should be first'. He was convinced that God had given him the task of "slay[ing] my enemies with their own weapons".

Nat Turner then led his fellow enslaved people into a rebellion in August 1831, killing between 55 and 65 people, 51 of which were white. This drove so much fear in their white owners that had it not been for the simple fact of numbers, Nat Turner and his group would have succeeded. After a few days, the rebellion was no more but Turner could not be found until two months afterwards.

The Nat Turner story started shattering all the pre- and misconceived ideas about black people – their level of intelligence, physical strength, and all other human parameters. Black people could think, strategize, innovate, and fight. All that strengthened the resolve of white people, now that blacks have been able to prove they have all the same qualities as they, the whites, to develop more stringent and inhuman ways to suppress blacks.

During the American Civil War, white Americans saw how tactful, and strong, blacks were especially in handling weapons. The fear that has been instilled in white Americans, will forever compel them not to modify the 2nd Amendment. The presence of blacks in America coupled with the inhuman, un-godly and wicked treatment of blacks without guidance from the Bible, will never allow whites in America to make any modification, however minuscule, to that amendment.

On December 14, 2014, Americans were once again told how a single gunman, Adam Lanza, shot and killed 26 people including 20 children between six and seven years, at the Sandy Hook Elementary School in Connecticut. Those who were privileged to see the pictures described how gruesome some were, to have been inflicted on human beings of that age. The President, Barack Obama, had tears run down his cheeks when narrating to the people of America. The story shook many people in the country and the wide world. There was wide speculation and hope that the Government would do something to control at least certain types of guns. The National Rifle Association – NRA, stood its ground and nothing came out of it. Mass gun killings have continued since them with no hope of control in sight. If anything were to be the catalyst for change, this would have been, but it has not. I do not think there will ever be.

In the whole of the Western world, gun possession is controlled by the states, so that mass killings with guns are rare. In Australia, on April 28 – 29 1996, there was a mass killing by a lone gunman in Port Arthur Tasmania, during which 35 people were killed and 23 wounded. That massacre prompted a severe crackdown on firearms during which more than 640,000 weapons were turned in and confiscated

In Maryland, a relatively quiet state, a day after President Barack Obama won the elections in 2008, gun and ammunition sales shot up about three to five times. How can one explain that? For me, it is white guilt and fear that blacks would feel emboldened to take up arms and retaliate the same reason white supremacists formed into militias to 'defend' themselves that has resulted in all the chaos in a state like Michigan where white supremacist groups stormed the governor's mansion and planned to kidnap and harm the governor.

To solve this problem of slave rebellion, the slave owners in the state of Virginia in 1712, requested the advice of longtime slave owner and consultant from the Caribbean, Willie Lynch. He was known to have implemented techniques that quelled the rebellious spirit of the slaves under his ownership. To describe the technics, I will give excerpts from the book *Post Traumatic Slavery Disorder* by Omar G Reid, PsyD; Sekou Mims, MEd, MSW, LCSW; and Larry Higginbottom, MSW and LCSW:

> Males: Take the meanest and most restless nigger, strip him of his clothes in front of the remaining male niggers, the female, and the nigger infant, tar and feather him, tie each leg to a different horse in opposite directions, set him a fire and beat both horses to pull him apart in front of the remaining niggers. The next step is to take a bullwhip and beat another nigger male to the point of death in front of the female and infant. Do not kill him.
>
> Females: Take a female, run a series of tests on her to see if she will submit to your desires willingly. Test her in every way because she is the most important of good economics. If she shows any signs of resistance in

submitting completely to your will, do not hesitate to use the bullwhip on her to extract the last bit of bitch out of her. Take care not to kill her, for in doing so you spoil good economics. When in complete submission, she will train her off-spring in the early years to submit to labor when they come of age.

Controlled Language: We must, completely, annihilate the mother tongue to both the new nigger and the new mule and institute a new language that involves the new life's work of both. You know language is a particular institution. It leads to the heart of the people. For example, you take slave, if you teach him all about your language, he will know all your secrets, and he is then no more a slave, for you cannot fool him any longer, and being a fool is one of the basic ingredients of and incidents to the maintenance of the slave system.

Children: A brief discourse in an offspring development will shed light on the key to sound economic principles. Pay little attention in the generation of original breaking but concentrate on future generations.

Willie Lynch assured the slave owners that, if they followed and adhered to his advice, they were surely going to be in control of not only the present crop of slaves but also future ones. The authors have asserted that the terrorism the slaves were subjected to has been the basis of the psychological trauma that was meant to be transmitted from one generation of slaves to the next, which is the main reason for their book. This they consider to be a psychiatric condition—posttraumatic slavery disorder, which is not yet agreed on by the American psychiatric body. The brutality was such that the verb *to lynch* appeared in American lingo to mean brutalize the slave/negro.

As a Black African living in the United States, I was always baffled by the docile attitude demonstrated by my African American colleagues at work as soon as a White official appeared. I now understand why, especially after all the unspeakable brutality exerted by White people on Black people. I have been asking myself, if we were created in the image of God, where has he been all the time such brutality was being exerted on his children? These people were Christians who had run away from prosecution in England, only to turn around, forget about their Christian teachings, and brutalize their fellow human beings. How valid is the Christian doctrine? Is it only for White people to use as they wish, using Christianity to justify slavery of people of a different color with all its brutality and annihilation or extermination of whole tribes in the Americas? What is the justification that Christianity has for slavery?

During the Holocaust, the Nazi doctors were performing experiments on Jewish women to prevent them from getting pregnant. Is the world not inadvertently bearing witness to same? The Israeli newspaper the Haaretz, published in its website that for the first time a government official acknowledged the practice of injecting Ethiopian women with Depo-Provera, against their will and without their knowledge. These women belong to the Falashas, believed to be Jews living in Ethiopia and airlifted to Israel in the 80s.

The Director General of the Ministry of health, Prof. Roni Gamzu, instructed the four health maintenance organizations to stop the practice, also all gynecologists in the HMOs, not to renew prescriptions for Depo-Provera if for any reason there is concern, they might not understand the ramifications of the treatment.

Benjamin Netanyahu, the hardline Prime Minister of Israel, had always denied he was racist. But what explanation can one derive from this policy? Why inject the women without their knowledge and or consent if the policy was a good one? Why the attempt to even think of controlling the birth rate? What are white Jews afraid of? Are there any bad memories of happenings between Jews and black Africans to provoke such a policy? The US powerful newspapers were somehow quiet on that news probably for fear of embarrassing their bosses or owners. This thus provokes memories of the Tuskegee experiment on black people for syphilis.

CHAPTER 4

Colonial Period

W hen the transatlantic slave trade ended, the European nations, especially the maritime ones turned their attention to Africa, which they considered uninhabited but somehow rich. For a long time, they had been baffled over what the continent was, based on all the derogatory descriptions given to them by early Christian missionaries. The land they occupied was full of untapped riches, which would bring enormous wealth to the Europeans nations.

During biblical times, extraordinarily little or nothing was known about Africa. The initial spread of Christianity as begun by Saul or Paul was limited to the Mediterranean basin and what is today known as the Middle East, as depicted by the epistles or letters addressed to the Assyrians, the Thessalonians, and other groups.

For the Europeans, Africa was a no-man's land—*res nullius*. The Portuguese were the most prominent of the slave traders. Having been given the permission by the Pope, they opened trading posts all along the west coast of Africa.

Before David Livingstone died, he called for a worldwide crusade to open Africa using what he called the three Cs—commerce, Christianity, and civilization (what I call the unholy trinity of trade, religion, and plunder). This thus opened the gateway for the mad rush to plunder and brutalize the people of Africa for centuries.

In this chapter, I want you as an African to see and understand how the religion of Christianity was used to soften Africans in a bid to prepare them for exploitation, plunder, and brutality.

King Leopold II, of all the European leaders, was the most eager to plunder Africa, based on all that he had been hearing from explorers like David Livingstone, Stanley, and others.

After the Berlin Conference of 1884, the heart of Africa was carved out and given to King Leopold II of Belgium. A letter he wrote to the missionaries he was sending to the now Congo served as a blueprint on how Europeans should treat Africans. It instructed:

> Reverends, Fathers and Dear Compatriots: The task that is given to fulfill is very delicate and requires much tact. You will go certainly to evangelize, but your evangelization must inspire above all Belgium interests. Your principal objective in our mission in the Congo is never to teach the niggers to know God, this they know already.
>
> They speak and submit to a Mungu, one Nzambi, one Nzakomba, and what else I do not know. They know that to kill, to sleep with someone else's wife, to lie and to insult is bad. Have courage to admit it; you are not going to teach them what they know already. Your essential role is to facilitate the task of administrators and industrials, which means you will go to interpret the gospel in the way it will be the best to protect your interests in that part of the world.
>
> For these things, you must keep watch on disinteresting our savages from the richness that is plenty [in their underground to avoid that, they get interested in it, and make you murderous] competition and dream one day to overthrow you. Your knowledge of the gospel will allow you to find texts ordering, and encouraging your followers to love poverty, like "Happier are the poor because they will inherit the heaven," and, "It's difficult for the rich to enter the kingdom of God." You must detach from them and make them disrespect

everything which gives courage to affront us. I refer to their Mystic System and their war fetish—warfare protection—which they pretend not to want to abandon, and you must do everything in your power to make it disappear. Your action will be directed essentially to the younger ones, for they will not revolt when the recommendation of the priest is contradictory to their parents' teachings.

The children must learn to obey what the missionary recommends, who is the father of their soul. You must singularly insist on their total submission and obedience, avoid developing the spirit in the schools, teach students to read and not to reason. There, dear patriots, are some of the principles that you must apply. You will find many other books, which will be given to you at the end of this conference. Evangelize the negroes so that they stay forever in submission to the white colonialists, so they never revolt against the restraints they are undergoing. Recite every day— "Happy are those who are weeping because the kingdom of God is for them."

Always convert the blacks by using the whip. Keep their women in nine months of submission to work freely for us. Force them to pay you in sign of recognition—goats, chicken, or eggs—every time you visit their villages. And make sure that niggers never become rich. Sing every day that it is impossible for the rich to enter heaven. Make them pay tax each week at Sunday mass. Use the money supposed for the poor, to build flourishing business centers. Institute a confessional system, which allows you to be good detectives denouncing any black that has a different consciousness contrary to that of the decision-maker. Teach the niggers to forget their heroes and to adore only ours. Never present a chair to a black that comes to visit you. Do not give him more than one cigarette. Never invite him for dinner even if he gives you a chicken every time you arrive at his house.

The above letter, which shows the real intention of the Christian missionary's journey in Africa, was exposed to the world by Mr. Moukouani Muikwani Bukoko, who was born in the Congo in 1915 and who, in 1935 while working in the Congo, bought a secondhand Bible from a Belgian priest who forgot the speech in the Bible. This was brought to academia by Dr. Chiedozie Okoro

This letter has exposed the hypocrisy, duplicity, and shamelessness of Europeans toward Africans. They knew that the message they would be delivering to the Africans was false and deceptive, but they went ahead with it anyway.

As the message was deliberately targeted toward the young generation, my message is also directed to the young Africans, who have been bamboozled into the ways of the Whiteman through Christianity as demonstrated by the flamboyant lifestyle of African pastors and bourgeoisie.

White missionaries are known to have explored Africa for decades before the Berlin Conference, where the agreement was arrived at to chop up the continent according to the needs of the respective powers. Information sent back to Europe by these missionaries was then used to execute the tasks eventually given to their respective emissaries. This can be seen in the letter written by King Leopold II, who was the most eager, most anxious, and readiest to go plunder the continent. They knew that Africans believed in God like Europeans, only through, according to King Leopold II, a Mungu, Nzambi, or Nzakomba. This is in direct contradiction of what Sir Samuel Baker said that "Without any exception they are without a belief in a Supreme Being. Neither have they any form of worship nor idolatry nor is the darkness of their minds enlightened by even a ray of superstition. The mind is as stagnant as the morass which forms its puny world."

I had always wondered if our forefathers ever resisted the new way of belief in God as they knew it. Well, I followed the advice of Professor Kofi Awoonor—to educate myself. I found a lot that has driven me to present my ideas for consideration and scrutiny, as Black people, Africans, must look back at both Christianity and Islam to find out whether their introduction was for their benefit or for that of those who introduced these religions to them. Why is it that, even when Black

Africans resisted the Europeans politically, they could not rid themselves of the European's religion, instead finding a way of accommodating it?

To convince the Africans, the Whiteman brought in the image of Jesus Christ, which is White in the context of the Holy Trinity—the Father, the Son, and the Holy Spirit. God was all of those, the Father and the Son and the Holy Spirit. For the first time, God had been given a face and flesh, something very strange to Africans, as they knew God was invisible. The White missionaries deliberately showed Jesus Christ as being as White as they were, making the Africans believe that the Whiteman was God in human flesh and that obeying these white missionaries meant obeying Mungu, Nzambi, or Nzakomba. This created a lot of confusion in the minds of Africans, as they strongly believed that God was now a human being with the color white.

King Leopold's letter is gold, as it contains all that Black Africans need to know about the Whiteman's intentions in Africa. He wrote in vivid terms what the missionaries should do to get the people to go along with the teachings from the missionaries: "You will go certainly to evangelize, but your evangelization must inspire above all Belgium interests. Your principal objective in our mission in the Congo is never to teach the niggers to know God, this they know already."

The contents of this letter have been applied all over the Black Africa that fell under European evangelization.

Showing the image of Jesus Christ as the Son of God to the Africans was most deceptive, as for them, God had no color and was perceived as a spirit. So how could he have a son or a daughter who was White? Such a controversial concept was a way of implementing the missionaries' instructions pertaining to the youth: "Your action will be directed essentially to the younger ones, for they won't revolt when the recommendation of the priest is contradictory to their parents' teachings."

After centuries of indoctrination and brainwashing, Black Africans have come to accept that concept readily because their parents before them had done so. They had to follow suit; and dare anybody to challenge them.

In recent years, the image of Jesus Christ as used by Europeans is being challenged by some Black theologians. A Ghanaian scholar came up with a theory that Jesus was Black; not many Black men paid attention. At another time, the lineage of Jesus Christ was talked about and traced to Abyssinia (in other words, Ethiopia). In 1984 and 1985, Israel airlifted the Black Jews or Falashas out of Ethiopia, thus giving credence to the saying that there were and are Blacks among the Jews.

Walter McCrae, a West Indian theologian, in his preaching about the Black presence in the Bible, claims that Abraham, Moses, Joshua, and Elijah were all Black. If it is said or claimed that Jesus descended from Abraham and he is Black, is there not the possibility that Jesus also was Black? Can it not also be argued that this was why he was not accepted by the Jews—under the pretext that he was not the Messiah they were expecting? When did the first picture of Jesus appear in the form it is portrayed today and by whom?

Walter McCrae and others are trying to accommodate Christianity, since the indoctrination is so deep in the psyche of Black people that some have decided to just accept and move on. But I disagree, as the mortar used as concrete is exactly that. Let Christians prove to the rest of us why Jesus is White and not Black as his father is the Holy Spirit.

To propagate their concepts, the missionaries opened schools and colleges to teach the children about Christianity, especially promoting teachings that were contrary to the beliefs of the older generation. The young people were made to understand that their ancestors believed in false gods. But who or what is a false god? *Oxford Dictionary* defines a god as a supernatural being or spirit and God spelt with a capital "G" as the creator of the universe. How can a spirit, which is not visible to humankind, be false? So, in the traditional African or Blackman's belief, there was no concept of a false god, as he knew only of one Supreme Being—God Almighty, hence his name in various languages.

Nobody has ever seen, and no one will ever see God Almighty. He is only in the perception and imagination of the individual or community, and it is that which is expressed in different ways by different people the world over (Blacks are not exempt). No Whiteman has ever seen God. Nor has any Whiteman died and come back from heaven or hell to tell humankind what he or she found there. But the Whiteman has used Christianity to arrogate to himself the power to dictate to the rest of the world how the world should be.

The Greeks believed in gods and superstition. And the philosophy they developed as a result was described as Greek mythology, which has been extensively studied. Why was it not described as primitive, like the Blackman's philosophy was?

Why was the skin color of Jesus Christ so important? The Catholic Church knew that presenting Jesus to the European pagans as a Jew would have been a tough sell. So, the Pope, at the time, requested that Michelangelo produce an artistic impression of Jesus Christ. Being an Italian, he produced an impression of a White male with long flowing hair and blue eyes.

This picture was used successfully to make Jesus acceptable to the rest of Europe. The picture was then used effectively by European missionaries in Africa and the rest of the world, including in South America to make the unsuspecting people accept that the Whiteman was God in the flesh. That caused a lot of confusion and consternation in the minds of Africans. So, the missionaries decided to concentrate on the children, as was initially advised by King Leopold II.

Africans grappled with this notion so much that after World War II, Simon Kimbangu from the Lower Congo posed the following question to the Belgian authorities: "If Jesus were to communicate with black people, did he need to do so through White missionaries?" For that he was prosecuted and sentenced to death; the sentence was later commuted to life imprisonment, and he spent more years in prison than Jesus spent on earth, just because, as a Blackman, his job was to listen and learn but not to have any ideas of his own except those brought to him from outside.

Amadu Bamba of Senegal, who started the Moureed Brotherhood was given the same treatment by the French, who exiled him for twelve years and succeeded in making him into a martyr.

Each one of the colonial powers adapted King Leopold's message according to the people and situation on the ground. In British West Africa, the Church Missionary Society (CMS) was the leading religious organization, as it represented the Church of England, followed by the Methodists and then the Catholic Church. As an arm of the Church of England, headed by the monarch, the CMS was the most influential and powerful. CMS missionaries opened the Fourah Bay College in

Freetown, Sierra Leone, to train pastors for the West African region, consisting of Nigeria, Ghana, Sierra Leone, and Gambia. Sierra Leone then became the center of British learning, training civil servants, teachers, pastors, and others.

That pattern was repeated in East and Central Africa, with Makerere University becoming the center of learning and production of pastors and civil servants for the promotion of British interests and culture.

The policy created a new crop of Africans who regarded themselves as successors to the colonialists, and as such, they claimed the same rights and privileges the system gave their former masters. These newly empowered Africans owed everything to the new religions of their masters and, having been indoctrinated into the systems of their masters, believed in their religion and all that it gave them. The African people thus became divided, not only through their colonial masters but also by class—the newly empowered and the rest of the population—as well as by Islam.

CHAPTER 5

The Coming of Islam

Islam came into Africa and, according to historical accounts, by way of Muslim refugees fleeing prosecution in the Arab peninsula. Seven years after peaceful coexistence, the locals were attacked and conquered in the seventh century CE after the death of the Prophet Muhammad in 639 CE.

From that period, Islam spread quickly along West Africa through merchants, traders, and scholars as African rulers themselves either tolerated by turning a blind eye or converted to Islam. To a large part, Islam mainly spread wherever there was trade to be made, especially where there were clusters of Muslims or those who just tolerated them. Indigenous beliefs and practices were tolerated with the acceptance of the rulers and, in some cases, even blended with the new religion.

As trade flourished in West Africa, so Islam spread from one empire to another, first in Gao in 985 CE and then within the Ghana Empire from the tenth century CE. The religion spread virtually through the rest of West Africa. Making things easier was the recognition by the African rulers that adopting Islam or at least tolerating it would be good for trade. Islam and trade were very intertwined, as well described in UNESCO's *General History of Africa*:

> The association of Islam and trade in sub-Saharan Africa is a well-known fact. The commercially most active peoples, the Dyula, Hausa and Dyakhanke, were among

the first to be converted when their respective countries met Muslims. The explanation of this phenomenon is to be found in social and economic factors. Islam is a religion born in the commercial society of Mecca and preached by a Prophet who himself had for a long time been a merchant, provides a set of ethical and practical prescripts closely related to business activities. This moral code helped to sanction and control commercial relationships and offered a unifying ideology among the members of different ethnic groups, thus providing for security and credit, two of the chief requirements of long-distance trade. (Vol. III, 39)

In the Ghana Empire, there was no inclination by the kings toward Islam. Rather, they tolerated the Muslim merchants and those wanting to practice the religion. But in the Mali Empire, the kings readily accepted and converted to Islam. Mansa Uli even went on pilgrimage to Mecca in the 1260s or 1270s CE. Many kings followed. Famous among them was Mansa Musa I, who ruled from 1312 to 1337 CE. He visited Cairo and Mecca, and it was he who brought back to Mali Muslim scholars, architects, and books. He consequently built the Great Mosque of Timbuktu and schools and universities. Among the clerics were Sudanese, who later went as missionaries, spreading Islam in the rest of West Africa.

For those kings who accepted Islam, on top of the riches trade gave them to help them maintain power, there was this idea of a new dynasty that the new religion brought. Islam also brought literacy, which helped the kings spread their messages and to hold on to power.

Not all the kings accepted Islam. King Sunni Ali of Songhai Empire refused Islam.

Most of the kings tolerated the practice of indigenous beliefs, especially in rural communities. But as Islamic studies were conducted in Arabic, that discouraged a lot of the people, excluding everyone except the educated clerical class of towns and cities. As a result, the Islam that emerged was of a particular variation, different from that practiced in the Arab world. This can be attributed to the fact that the African rulers were not able to completely dismiss the religious practices and beliefs of most of their people, which often elevated their rulers to divine or semidivine status. For all these reasons, Islam was absorbed into many indigenous practices, making it much easier for the people to accept—unlike Christianity, which came with a tabula rasa, a deliberate effort to completely change the identity of the people. Polygamy is accepted in Islam, as well as immediate burial after death.

Islam easily spread from the Arabian Peninsula, to the east coast of Africa, mainly by way of traders, who started settling among the indigenous people, creating permanent settlements along the Swahili coast. Intermarriages started, thus blending cultural practices, which led to the evolution of a unique Swahili culture.

It was not all smooth sailing, as Islam entered a fierce competition with Christianity in places like Nubia, Faras, Dongola, and Alodia in what is today Ethiopia.

The mass adoption of Islam by Africans was preceded by a long period of coexistence, with Islam maintaining a minority status and not threatening the status quo. In many regions of Africa, Islam has gradually taken the place of traditional religions, sometimes with external help but mostly without violence.

CHAPTER 6

Abuse of African Religious Beliefs

Now that both religions found their respective places in the societies they lived in; the deceit of Africans went into full gear.

As I have explained earlier, our ancestors did not need or have prophets, as they believed they had a link with God through their deities. But the missionaries started telling them that their ancestors had believed in false gods, showing them the image of Jesus Christ as part of the Holy Trinity of the Father, the Son, and the Holy Spirit to prove their point. That created confusion in the minds of the Africans, as God, in their knowledge and belief, was not a human being to be seen but a spirit that lived everywhere among them.

So, in the traditional African or Blackman's belief, there was no concept of a false god, as he knew only of one Supreme Being—God Almighty, hence his name in various languages.

Nobody has ever seen nor will ever see God Almighty. He is only in the perception and imagination of the individual or community. And it this perception that is expressed in different ways by different people the world over, the Blackman being no exception. Nobody, white, black, brown, yellow, Chinese, Japanese, or of any creed or ethnicity— and no Whiteman—has died and come back from heaven or hell to tell humankind what he or she saw there. But the Whiteman has used Christianity to arrogate to himself the power to dictate to the rest of the world as to how the world should be.

The European who believes in God also believes that praying to God through Jesus Christ will get him or her to the salvation sought but condemns the African, whose ancestors were the first *Homo sapiens* in this world, for praying to the same God through his or her own deities. What an arrogance. The Muslim uses the name of Muhammad as Messenger of God, just as the Buddhists go through Buddha, the Japanese through Shinto, and the Hindis through their thousands of mini gods to reach God Almighty, with little or no criticism from Europeans who have spread Christianity around the world. The Greeks believed in gods, and the philosophy they developed as a result was described as Greek mythology. Why was it not described as primitive, like the Blackman's was? How did it come to even be studied widely in literature while the Blackman's was not?

The deception of the African peoples is so glaring in King Leopold II's letter in which he clearly stated:

> Your essential role is to facilitate the task of administrators and industrials, which means you will go to interpret the gospel in the way it will be the best to protect your interests in that part of the world. For these things, you must keep watch on disinteresting our savages from the richness that is plenty [in their underground ...
>
> Your knowledge of the gospel will allow you to find texts ordering, and encouraging your followers to love poverty, like "Happier are the poor because they will inherit the heaven" and, "It is difficult, for the rich to enter the kingdom of God."

These ideas were enforced on the people using administrative and political might and, most important of all, education of the younger generation through the establishment of schools and universities.

The European brought Christianity, showing Jesus Christ as the Son of God but at the same time telling the Blackman that God is invisible, which the Blackman knew, and that God is also the Holy Spirit, which the Blackman, by inference, also knew.

The European said that the Holy Trinity was God the Father, the Son, and the Holy Ghost, and that the Bible also said that the Virgin Mary had Jesus Christ through virgin birth, having become pregnant through the power of the Holy Spirit, and the product was Jesus Christ. How come Jesus is White, when the Holy Spirit has no color, as nobody has ever seen him? Christians accept this wholeheartedly as part of the mysticism and therefore faith, and they dare anybody to challenge them. Muslims do not accept it, but both condemn the Blackman for what he believes in that it has no reference to either Jesus or Muhammad. Black people have inadvertently been drawn into squabbles not of their making and have been damaging each other as a result.

In an earlier chapter, I explained how the image of Jesus was particularly important to the early Church in her narration of the story of Jesus to the pagans of Europe. As it was important that time, it was even more important this epoch, as the recipients of the image were different. The image as presented to the Africans rendered a twofold advantage: 1. It facilitated their accepting Jesus Christ as part of the Holy Trinity 2. It established the supremacy of the Whiteman through Jesus.

King Leopold II made things much easier for the missionaries when he told them, "Your action will be directed essentially to the younger ones, for they will not revolt when the recommendation of the priest is contradictory to their parents' teachings. The children must learn to obey what the missionary recommends, who is the father of their soul. You must singularly insist on their total submission and obedience, avoid developing the spirit in the schools, teach students to read and not to reason." This was a success for them, as the use of the word "father" in respect of the priests, made the children erroneously believe that the priests were replacing their fathers and, as such, were to be obeyed.

The missionaries were further told, "Your knowledge of the gospel will allow you to find texts ordering, and encouraging your followers to love poverty, like 'Happier are the poor because they will inherit the heaven' and, 'It is difficult for the rich to enter the kingdom of God.' You have to detach from them and make them disrespect everything which gives courage to affront us."

This was very cleverly done as the children who were growing up poor and had, never seen riches, readily accepted that preaching. This bore more weight when the Muslims also were preaching that the afterlife was more important than this, in which they lived. Most Africans do believe that being poor is a virtue, so seeing White people taking away their riches never provoked resentment in them—until the Whiteman became arrogant in his political treatment of their Black subjects.

One myth that the missionaries sold nicely to Africans is that Jesus Christ died to save humankind. Really? My problem with that is that there is nothing in the Bible or narratives about Jesus to suggest that he ever knew about the existence of Black people—if we should believe the image as portrayed by the Church. Jesus was also a Jew, who never liked the way his people were treated and eventually rose to save them from Roman rule. There is also no evidence that his disciples knew about Black people, as there is no reference about us in any of their letters or epistles. This convoluted logic is what Africans have been subjected to; and they have been made to believe that it is sinful to challenge that idea. Young developing African brains were made to believe what they were fed without question.

Way back in the 1960s, many of our parents' residences, Muslim, or Christian, were decorated with pictures of Adam and Eve standing with a tree bearing apples between them and a snake hanging over them. The picture was meant to demonstrate the story of the original sin. What the picture did not tell us is why they were White and not Black and who was there to have seen them as White and not Black? Black Africans who have accepted Christianity easily dismiss the challenge by saying that one must have faith to believe it. Accepting that concept means one has accepted the superiority of the white color using Christianity. Who was there to see Adam and Eve as White? The idea is good to the unsuspecting African, believing he or she is Christian. All these ideas were/are deceptive, making the African submissive to the supremacy of the Whiteman through Christianity, and the Arab through Islam.

And once the African had bought into all this deception, the unrelenting plunder of the continent of Africa was on its way.

The concept of Satan is another confusing aspect of the global deception of the Black African. Nobody has ever seen Satan, but why is he always shown as Black? What is the significance of that? Is there a word for Satan in Black African languages as the name God is in every African language independent of each other? No, because it was a concept that was new to our people and, as such, had, until now, not had a proper place in our people's vocabulary.

Let us look at it this way. Jesus Christ has been shown as White and as God the Son. To anchor the belief of Christians, the concept of Satan had to be brought in as evil and Black. No Black African language had a separate word for Satan, as that concept was not in the minds of Africans. Our people knew about witches and their powers, traditional healers, charms, and the sorcerer or clairvoyant. Each Black African language had a separate word for God totally independent of the other but none for Satan. The name for Satan is the same in virtually every African language, with varying pronunciations. By accepting the concept of Satan as Black and evil, the Black African was inadvertently accepting that he or she was inferior and evil, exactly the way the Whiteman looked at the Blackman.

In Islam, Muhammad has not been made visible, as no picture of him has been available although he appeared some centuries after Jesus. He is believed by Muslims to be an Arab. The role of the Blackman in the Quran has not been made explicit and Black Islamic theologians have not made any attempt in such studies because they have been made to believe that it is blasphemous. Muslims I have spoken to say that the first call to prayer was made by a Blackman, a slave named Bilal, which is not sufficient to show the role of Black people in Islam during the days of the prophet Muhammad. The vast majority of Black Africans cannot read Arabic, much less Quranic Arabic, so they swallow—hook, line, and sinker—all they are told by whomsoever claims to know the Quran. For example, Black people are told that we originated from Egypt and that we are offshoots from Arabs. This is startling, and no educated Blackman, not even educated Egyptians, will accept such an untruth. Such a statement inherently proves that the Blackman is inferior to the Arab, and history has proven otherwise. Meanwhile, both religions preach equality of the races in the sight of God.

As we have seen so far, Christianity had the power of politics behind it, coupled with the extensive privileges given to its converts. Christianity entered stiff competition with Islam in all the countries that both entered and overpowered Islam in our countries because of the respective European power of their origin—for example, the English and the Anglican Church and the French, Spanish, and Portuguese and Catholicism.

Colonialism made Islam occupy a secondary position, as the levers of power were dominated by Christianity. This is true in the Middle East and Arab North Africa.

Whereas Christianity was used to subdue the Blackman and to force him to submit to the supremacy of the Whiteman, Islam not only kept the Blackman in his ignorance and kept him from searching for more knowledge, but it also made him feel second class to the Arab. Muslims were told that to send a child to school was to make him into an unbeliever. So many children of Muslim parentage were prevented from attending school. Both religions tried and obliterated the past of Africans, especially those who believed in both religions. They were thus rendered naked and unattached. It was like hunting a baby baboon by shooting the mother and leaving the child at the mercy of the hunter, who can then command it to go in whichever direction he wants, although he will remain a baboon. So, the Blackman has been left at the mercy and whims and caprices of the hunter—the Arab or the European. We see it in the class struggle that ensued in African countries after independence, so eloquently written about by the late Dr. Kwame Nkrumah, first president of the Republic of Ghana, and IMF and the World Bank, who fervently believe that the Blackman cannot do anything right unless he is supervised.

The Blackman was stripped of his past, his beliefs, and the steerage of his own future, and made to follow the methods of the educator. Dr. Mouttolle of Union Minière in the then Congo, said, in an interview with Basil Davidson in 1946, "The Colonizer, must never lose sight of the fact that Negroes have the minds of children, minds, which are shaped by the methods of the educator, they look and listen, tell and imitate, the European must in all circumstances show himself a calm and thoughtful chief, good without weakness, benevolent without familiarity, active by method and, above all just, in the repression of faults as in the reward of good will."

This was the attitude in, Mother Africa, and it was very reminiscent of the attitude in the Americas, where the slaves were brutalized and deliberately stripped of their past, their beliefs, and all that made them also creations of God and then made to follow the ways dictated by their slave masters. They assumed the names and religion of their slave masters, and this has been with them ever since, leaving them with their Blackness. Despite all those efforts to force them to accept Christianity, the slaves were still not accepted as human beings, even when they established their own churches.

How can a slave master who could not allow his slave to sit at a table with him turn around and tell that very slave to follow him in the path of Jesus Christ so that they could share the Kingdom of God? If the slave master knew the latter was true, he would never have explained it to the slave or given him that privilege. Black churches have long been vandalized in the United States, especially during the presidency of Bill Clinton and very recently in Washington DC when one of the oldest churches for black people, the Ashbury United Methodist Church was vandalized by the Proud Boys, a supremacist hate group.

One would expect that preaching the word of Christ to Blacks was done to enable them to be accepted in the worldwide Christian community and to change all such attitudes towards Blacks. That has never happened. Why? I frankly believe that Whites who preach the word of God or Jesus Christ to Africans are deceitful, for they are using the Bible or the Quran to promote their self-interest, which is against the will of God and, as such, a sin. Black people have been found to be the most forgiving people God has created; otherwise, when Nelson Mandela and the ANC came to power in South Africa, wholesale retaliatory massacres of Whites would have taken place. Were they afraid of the United States or Britain or France or Germany? Plain and simple, no. Blacks are forgiving people.

CHAPTER 7

Effect of Foreign Domination on Africans

One thing that is intriguing for me is that, despite all that Blacks have suffered at the hands of White people and Arabs because of their religion, Black people still cling to these religions. One would expect that, after African nations became independent and Blacks attained freedom from slavery, they would revert to their ancestral roots—like the Algerians did after their civil war by transforming French churches to libraries and other establishments.

In Africa, the Blackman has tried to emulate the Whiteman by trying to change his accent, his style of dress, donning Western suits in hot weather; and his name and even going to stay among the Whites to copy them from within their society—all to no avail. There are some Black intellectuals who use classical music to show their level of sophistication. On the contrary, Black African musicians in the diaspora complain that they are also rebuffed from classical music and that black female bodies are not well structured to suit ballet dancing. Some say it is a matter of taste, but I hotly contest that because accepting somebody else's culture in preference to yours is so self-defeating that one's very existence becomes questionable. When Sir Ernest Beoku-Betts of Sierra Leone asked the British government in 1918 whether "the color of a man's skin is to make any difference within the Empire" and called for "equality of the races," the British Government through the Ormsby-Gore pronouncement of 1916, restated its position that, "The English man has naturally an instinctive dislike of 'assimilation'. We like to keep our life distinct from that of other races European or not. The more another people acquire our culture, our outlook, and social habits; very often the wider becomes the gulf between us ... We frequently get on better with people different from us, and we appreciate the differences more than the points we have in common" (Professor Akintola Wyse, *The Krio of Sierra Leone: An Interpretive History*). This was British arrogance being expressed when the empire was booming. This just means that, if you do not accept your identity—in other words, the way you are—he will not accept you; in other words, you will be lost like a satellite in space. African musicians go to Europe to record and market their music to avoid piracy back home. But in the process, the beats and taste are modified to suit European audiences.

The Blackman has been so indoctrinated that he associates anything good or beautiful with White or near White (mulatto). And the Whiteman, seeing the eagerness of Blacks to be White, made skin lightening or bleaching creams to further fool the Blackman and woman. Francophone intellectuals are guiltier of this than are their Anglophone counterparts. One goes to conferences and sees Francophone intellectuals in Western suits as if they have nothing national to put on to mark their identity.

I am sure that President Mobutu had this in mind in 1972 when he came up with his policy of 'authenticité' after he quarreled with the Catholic Church. That meant that all industries in Zaire/Congo were to be nationalized, although with disastrous consequences and most important, that all Zairean/Congolese Christians were to be baptized with Zairean/Congolese names. He started by changing his own name from Joseph Desire Mobutu to Mobutu Sese Seko Kuku Ngbendu wa Za Banga and his style of dress. Why was this necessary? Well, to prove to foreign religious leaders that a person's name does not reflect on his or her belief in God.

The Blackman (African) goes to the Western world, accepts the Western style of life, and decries his own society as underdeveloped, corrupt, and a society that relegates women to the dustbin. An example is the massive brain drain that has seriously affected African societies and the consequent destruction of African families, with disastrous consequences for the children. Black marriages contracted at home mostly break up when couples transplant to the Western world and are exposed to Western ways of life, which are mostly contrary to what should identify them. Husband and wife divorce with mostly fatal consequences. It becomes brother against brother, sister against sister, daughter pushing mother out of the house, and son doing the same to father—things that are anathema to the African way of life. Children born of Black parents in the Western world grow up thinking White, doing White. They end up looking Black but being White inside, with little or no connection with their land of origin.

Can these children fit in our societies? What about Whites born in Black societies? Why don't they inculcate Black habits or think Black? Well, because the Blackman is to listen and learn and imitate. As the world is changing, a glimmer of light at the end of the cultural tunnel is starting to show. And it is beginning to wake up young Africans of immigrant parentage with a lure that urges them back to the motherland to build it.

In traditional African marriages, divorce was not that easy to come by. Couples seeking divorce might be frustrated by constant intervention of relatives—all in the name of and for the sake of the children, if any, within the wedlock. But with colonial intervention, marriages contracted in the church and by civil means received the full backing of the law. Divorces went through the courts of law, whereas marriages contracted by most Blacks, especially in Sierra Leone (in other words, by native law and custom) got just a gentle tap on the back from the law but no recognition of divorce in the courts.

This has thus created in those who contracted marriages in the churches and by civil means a feeling of superiority over those who married by other methods, thereby relegating marriage by native law and custom to insignificance, instead of developing and strengthening it. Fortunately, marital laws in, for example, Sierra Leone, have been revised, giving them equal recognition under the law, especially those of native law and custom.

Since independence, truly little was done to officially maintain the way of life and governance our ancestors lived by. It was only after the genocide in Rwanda that the traditional legal system that had governed the people for centuries before the coming of the European was used and restored. Rwanda today stands out as the single African country that has earned the respect of the rest of the world for its authentic way of doing things.

As Professor Kofi Awoonor said, five hundred years of indoctrination and brainwashing have made the African bourgeoisie believe that he or she is inferior to the Whiteman and all that the Whiteman stands for. Copying of Whites has caused such stagnation in the minds of Blacks that even the educated Blacks do not know where they are. I remember growing up in Sierra Leone and as young boys we were using white female beauty statistics like 30-24-32 to assess the beauty of our own girls. It was a pleasant surprise for me, after having been in Europe for so many, to have heard late President Jerry Rawlings of Ghana, express dismay at those black Africans who were using European female beauty statistics as a yardstick to assess the beauty of black African women. I am told that he even made beauty contests to be conducted using African/Ghanaian beauty statistics.

In the US, there was consternation among African Americans when young black Rappers were encouraged by producers to come up with lyrics demeaning black women. According to their producers the music sold. Black leaders could not have any of it and rightly so as these are black women/mothers who brought them forth into this world, also their sisters and aunts and cousins and grandmothers all of whom must be protected, respected, and loved not demeaned. That genre of music thankfully has faded away.

Again, how committed is the Blackman to these religions? My belief is that the Blackman is never committed to these religions except what he gets out of them prestige or dignity. Let us take the slaves in the Americas. The ones in the Caribbean, knowing full well they could not be allowed to openly practice their religion, decided to use deities that corresponded in importance to the saints of the Catholic Church and celebrated the same respective holidays as their slavers. The holiday of St. Luke, for example, would be celebrated with one of their deities, and the slavers all the time thought the slaves were celebrating the feast or holiday of the saints with them. That lasted for almost two hundred years before the slave masters finally caught up with the slaves, realizing what was really happening. It is said that the religion of Santeria, practiced in Cuba, and Kandumble in Brazil were born this way as well.

In the United States of America, the slaves had little option but to accept the religion of their slavers. Having gone through all the hardships of learning to read and write, they resorted to praying to God using Christianity. One would think that, with the slaves accepting and opening their own churches, the Christian community would accept them finally. No, it never worked that way, as the very Christian heads found chapters and verses in the Bible to justify their continued brutality against the Black slaves. The slaves turned to the church for salvation, for fellowship, and for spiritual satisfaction. The church, for them, meant everything, as it brought people together in strength and belief that, one day, they would be free. Unfortunately for the slaves, they were not to form groups of any size, as that constituted a threat to their slavers—who were forever in fear of them, as they knew what they were doing to a creation of God was not good in the sight of God. The White Christians started burning Black churches. This, to me, then means that all they were preaching was a lie, meant to hold the slaves in perpetual bondage—just like the preaching of the Europeans who came to Africa, deceiving Africans into Christianity.

The Black African does not care much about the duplicity in his adherence to both Christianity or Islam and his belief in ancestral worship and belonging to a secret society. How does the Blackman reconcile belief in God through Jesus or Muhammad and submission to his secret society? Most of the time he does not realize it, except when called on it. This is where the dilemma manifests itself very glaringly. Black Africans can go to church or mosque, quote verses fluently from the Bible or the Quran, but they will still go where their hearts belong.

Why should the Blackman divide himself like that? Can't a way be found for an African image to be created and accepted? Should the African intellectual alienate himself from the people he was born among and grew up among because of his newfound education? Some say it is because of poverty, but I say *no*. It is because of what Chief Emeka

Anyaoku, 3rd secretary-general of the Commonwealth, said—that "after independence Africans were in a haste to forget their past." Who told the Blackman to use politics to enrich himself? Who told the Blackman to be dishonest? The very Black men who use their education to look low on their people and exploit them even worse than the colonialists did. The very Black or African intellectual who preaches tribalism whenever he runs short of convincing ideas, thereby splitting his people, and causing long-lasting disunity. Examples are many. The Black or African intellectuals have been propagators of European and Arab conceptions of their color—of the idea that we cannot govern ourselves—all because Christianity and Islam are both trying, if not almost succeeding, to obliterating the Blackman's past.

Many African tribes have secret societies that give them identity, protection, hierarchy, and respect. The voodoo, which the Western world with its Christianity hated so much, held Haitians together to defeat the mighty army of the French in the 1800s. The Mau Mau in Kenya was used to achieve independence for Kenya. Some early missionaries refused to accept members of secret societies into their fold. For them to be accepted, they had to first renounce their allegiance to their secret societies to cut them off from their Blackness. Those who agreed to be converted turned around and criticized their own societies as evil and devilish, becoming, thereby, agents of self-destruction. These are happenings that go on till date, with the proliferation of new churches, each one targeting African religion just to get continued external financial support—just as Whites will always target Blacks to keep their societies going.

If we take a Black man who belongs to a secret society and is a Christian, he has been baptized twice and confirmed twice. But how? Before he becomes a Christian, he is initiated into the society and then confirmed as a member and given tribal marks indicative of the secret society. He then becomes a Christian. He is again baptized and confirmed a second time. No European Christian becomes baptized and confirmed twice.

In my discussions with people on this point, reference is always made to Masonic lodges in Europe, which they always take as superior to the secret societies of Black Africans. My response to that is these are societies that bring people of similar interests and tastes together for their own financial betterment. An example is Propaganda Due (P2), a Masonic lodge in Italy. P2 was embroiled in a lot of scandals, including corruption that led to the collapse of the Banco Ambrosiano, along with the disgraceful death in 1982 of Roberto Calvi, their president in London under the Blackfriars Bridge.

How also does the Blackman reconcile his belief in God through Jesus and Muhammad and his belief in the psychic or clairvoyant or marabou? Which one is much closer to him or typifies him? For the European/American, a clairvoyant is somebody who sees clearly into someone's fortunes. The Whiteman accepts astrologers, although the world and science has refused to accept astrology—the study of the stars in relation to the fortunes of humans—as a science. President Reagan believed very strongly in his astrologer, but when former President Mathew Kerekou of Benin believed and obeyed his astrologer or clairvoyant/psychic, he was rebuked by the Pope and mocked by, among others, his fellow Black men. African politicians go to the clairvoyant/psychic or marabou for the same reasons as French politicians have started using African clairvoyants/psychics. For them, it is acceptable. But for the Blackman, it is primitive and superstitious.

The late French President, Jacques Rene Chirac once said, "We bled Africa for four and a half centuries. We looted their raw materials, then we told lies that the Africans are good for nothing. In the name of religion, we destroyed their culture. And after being made rich at their expense, we now steal their brains through miseducation and propaganda to prevent them from enacting Black retribution against us."

There is the case of an Islamic scholar at Fourah Bay in Sierra Leone who wanted to use his newfound Islamic belief to change his people's tradition from a secret society called Orjeh, to strict adherence to Islam. He was rejected on the grounds that (1) he was born in it, and (2) that was part of their society and belief. What a dilemma!

Fourah Bay is situated in the eastern part of Freetown where those freed slaves of Muslim belief settled. They are mostly from the west coast of Africa; some say mainly Nigeria as their names depict mostly Yoruba language. The language of their secret society is also mainly Yoruba and/or Igbo. The secret society has long been the mortar that held them together, hence the resistance.

The Dilemma of the Blackman (African) is further demonstrated during the month of Ramadan, especially in the Mano River countries (Guinea, Sierra Leone, and Liberia), when the sale of alcohol suddenly drops, to go up again suddenly the day it ends. Is it that the Christians also join with Muslims to fast or is it that Muslims, despite the ban on the consumption of alcohol, drink alcohol? Interestingly, in Chinua Achebe's *Arrow of God*, when Ezeulu would receive a guest at his home, after the initial niceties, he would call on his wife to bring kola nuts and palm wine to welcome the guest. Christianity and Islam then divided the people in a culture that united them. The Christians encouraged their followers to drink wine as palm wine and refused kola nuts, whereas the Muslims discouraged theirs from drinking wine as palm wine, as the religion bans it, but encouraged them to eat kola nuts. In Arab lands, the Muslims were encouraged to drink coffee rather than alcohol. This aspect of the people's culture is prevalent till today.

The Blackman has been made to dance to the tune of outsiders and whenever that tune is played, he dances to it almost to a trance and will even be ready to kill his fellow Blackman for that. Where were Jesus and Muhammad when Africans were being taken and sold as slaves? Why didn't they intervene at Goree Island and all along the west coast of Africa, where the slaves were assembled and sorted out and labeled like animals? Where was humanity and all this talk that we are all creations of the one God when Black children were forcibly taken away from their mothers and homelands and shipped away to the Americas? Have White people apologized? Former President Bill Clinton, who many Blacks believe to be their friend, missed that opportunity to apologize. President George W. Bush also avoided apologizing for all that cruelty against members of God's family. The simple reason is that they still believe innately that Blacks are inferior, irrespective of that the fact that Colin Powell and Condoleezza Rice, both Blacks, were in the cabinet of the most powerful government in the world.

Religious fundamentalism has grown rapidly among our younger folks—so much so that those in our higher institutions of learning go about campuses with Bibles in hand expecting miracles, instead of paying more attention to the reasons for their being there. As a result, some of them, and the number is increasing, fall by the wayside, and the cumulative effect of this will certainly be disastrous for Africa.

Is the Blackman ready for such an eventuality? I pray that it does not happen, for it is easier to put up one Blackman against the other using these religions and tribalism than to get Black men together for economic and social development. The amount of energy spent by Black men trying to be what they are not supposed to be or what they are cajoled into is amazing and incredible. If all that energy had been spent on adult literacy campaigns to enlighten the masses about their conditions of life and how to improve on their lot, much would have been achieved. After all, these two religions never developed the world to what it is today; it is technology that has done so. And they both benefit from it. Since pre-independence African leaders disappeared from the scene, Africa lost its moral and political direction. It is also said that since Martin Luther King Jr. was killed, African Americans lost a rallying leader and, as such, lost leadership, and direction, thus compounding the many difficult problems inherent in the society. This is evidenced when one listens to Sirius XM channel 124, Joe Madison, "the Black Eagle." Listening to him over years, gave me a lot of insight into African American history and daily life.

In Nigeria, Black men are ready to tear each other apart more swiftly for these two religions than for economic reasons. In Cote D'Ivoire, what seemed to be submerged during Houphouet Boigny's reign came out and shook its ugly head in the open, resulting in a civil and tribal war between the Muslim north and the Christian south. In Sudan for years, the Muslim north imposed its religious will on the Christian south, which eventually led to the partition of Sudan and creation of South Sudan. All this was happening while those who spread these religions sat quietly and watched us, while they traded among themselves and planned how to keep us distracted from development with wars. While America, a de facto Christian state, protects Saudi Arabia, the custodian of all Muslim shrines, the Blackman is tearing his fellow Blackman apart for something that he has been forced to accept by these very people. For whom did Jesus Christ really die? Did he die to save the Jews from brutal Roman rule or for those in the Mediterranean basin or for the people south of the Sahara? Blacks were told, by the very people who held them as slaves, that he died for all humankind. What is the truism in that statement?

Even when the Second Vatican Council (1962–1965) issued the Lumen Gentium, a document meant to change the attitude of the Catholic Church toward Islam, a sort of rapprochement, that information was never spread around the African Muslim world. As a result of that document, there was the official visit made by the President of the Office for Non-Christian Affairs at the Vatican to Late King Faisal of Saudi Arabia in the course of 1974. Most important of all, was the fact that His Grace Bishop Elchinger received the Grand Ulema at his Cathedral in Strasbourg and invited them during their visit to pray in the choir. They did that before the altar turned toward the Mecca—what a rethink!

Why should Black men fight each other for Christianity and Islam? Why cannot Blacks understand that economic development and social cohesion will never be attained when they tear each other apart for these religions? Some people have replied that it will never happen. Fine, but Blacks are known to be nonchalant in the face of adversity, until it begins to crash on their heads. So, we are again becoming nonchalant to religious extremism until we begin to see brother fighting brother, father fighting son, and on and on—so much so that religious tolerance disappears completely. Whom will we then blame—the Whiteman?

The battle between Christianity and Islam was already started through the guise of looking for weapons of mass destruction and the removal from power of Saddam Hussein. The vast majority of Muslims in Africa pay little attention to or do not even know what is happening in the Islamic world. Many just do not bother to know the differences between Shiite and Sunni. All they know is they are all Muslims.

Pope John Paul II criticized President Nicephore Soglo, for attempting to worship like his ancestors—the voodoo way? Equally so, Rastafarianism, which I consider to be a protest religion, and its accompanying reggae music, have been vehemently cried down by both religions because:

1. The Rastafarians refer to Haile Selassie as their messiah.
2. During their daily ventures, they smoke ganja.

3. The Blackman should not have his own beliefs, adopting only those brought to him from outside.
4. It might be a rallying religion for Blacks.

Jose M. de Mesa, professor in the Mary Hill School of Theology in the Philippines, in his Contribution to the 62ⁿᵈ Yoko Civilization International Conference in Takayama Japan, said, "While no one religious tradition contains all the knowledge and wisdom regarding 'what it means to be human' in the world, each one has insights to offer towards the realization of our humanity as part of giving concrete shape to a total vision of being and becoming human, it is useful to listen and to learn from every religion regarding our humanity. After all, there is no ready-made plan to execute to be human."

Both Christians and Muslims claim that "divine" authority to preach or dictate to humankind how humankind should behave. And one may bear me witness that each time there is a talk with a Christian, he or she will try to persuade you to believe that the only way for humanity's salvation is through his or her own way of worship, and if one does not know the Bible, one is totally lost. The Muslims claim that their religion is the chosen religion of God and that the only way to God is through their belief.

The Blackman is faced with religious politics that has torn him apart. What about other peoples on earth who have no knowledge of either of these religions? Are they all doomed to hell? Well, religious fanatics on either side of the spectrum will give a categorical and emphatic *yes*. But how do they know? Can it be understood that, religiously, God put humankind in different geographic locations and created ways for each to pray to and worship him as he has prescribed. Religions like Buddhism, Hinduism, Shintoism, and others had been practiced for centuries, if not millennia, before Judaism, Christianity, and Islam arose.

In Africa, where the first humans appeared, the people had their own religion, which exists till today but under severe pressure, through which they prayed and worshipped God. Since Christianity and Islam started being practiced on earth and their followers saw how they could use these religions to dominate others, there has not been peace on this earth. In Africa, Christianity was backed by politics and raw colonial power, forcing the people to accept any deceitfulness inherent in them—telling the people to close their eyes when praying so that, by the time they opened their eyes something was missing from among them and using the preaching in the Bible to preach that, when your enemy gives you a slap on the right cheek, you turn the left cheek. These teachings made the Africans understand and believe that whatever the Whiteman did wrong to them physically, they should not retaliate.

But the Whiteman was mistaken. Their arrogance sold them out by their treatment; as is said in some African languages, "A joke is a joke, but putting pepper in a monkey's behind, is no joke, as he will fight back." Africans eventually realized that the pepper was too much, and rather than turn the other cheek, they turned around with an AK-47 (Anatoly Kalashnikov 1947).

Africans were made to believe that, as Muslims, they should eat only "halal" meat—in other words, meat from an animal that has been slaughtered by hand by cutting the throat of the animal, which should be healthy, with invocation of the name of God. The confusion or deceit in this idea is that most of the animals for consumption in the lands where Islam came from—arid desert lands—are domesticated. Most Black Africans, on the other hand, lived in the tropics, with massive forests, where many different animals were used for food by hunting them down. Wild animals are not—cannot be—caught and slaughtered as decreed by the religion (even animals as small as the rodent known as grasscutter). Africans were used to drinking wine free from the palm tree and eating meat from the forests, as that was what the Almighty God had provided for them. But then these two religions came and divided them into items that they paid little or no attention to.

In my part of Africa, West Africa, the Muslims had been told that they should not eat pork? But why? The explanation given them as narrated by many that I met was that, in the desert when it was difficult to get water, it was the pig or swine who showed the Prophet Muhammad where water was. From that time, the prophet prohibited the slaughter of the pig for food. My research showed me something totally different. In the Middle East, where the three religions emanated starting with Judaism and then Christianity and Islam, coming some two to three centuries later, Judaism, being the first of them, declared the pig or swine a filthy animal not suitable for human consumption. With the advent of Islam and the followers eating swine, the Jews started mocking them for eating a filthy animal. So, the Muslims were then banned from eating swine. Whatever the true story, the individual will choose which to believe.

God created the universe and, according to all three religions, all that lives on it. How can God tell one set of children to eat this type of food while banning others from doing so? The Muslims ban alcohol, as it will interfere with the five daily prayers. For the Jews, swine is filthy. But to tell African Muslims that the pig showed the prophet where water was in the desert is not tangible. When a very senior Muslim cleric was asked once on the BBC why Muslims should not eat pork, his reply was that the swine is a filthy animal. When asked about swine grown in special farms, he got annoyed and repeated his original answer. One can see that there is no tangible religious reason not to eat pork. If a Christian can eat pork and hopes to get to the Kingdom of God, why should a Muslim go to hell for eating same? Who is correct?

Nicolaus Copernicus, a Polish national, astronomer, and mathematician who lived in the time of the Renaissance in Europe, first postulated, and proved that the earth is round and rotates around its axis. This means that the earth is round, and as such, the whole of the earth cannot get sunlight or darkness at the same time, but the sky can be seen from any point on earth whether night or day. God is omnipotent and omnipresent and can be reached from any point one dies. So, it is also possible that somebody dying in Tokyo at night when it is daytime in Africa can get to God without coming through Africa? And if he is not Christian or Muslim, as most Japanese are, does he go to heaven or to hell, even when he believes very much in God through Shinto?

If no one religion can claim the monopoly on what it means to be human, why should the Blackman be dictated to? If each religion has its insights to offer its practitioners, why should the religions of the black people not be able to do so? Anthropology has proved beyond reasonable doubt that humans, as *Homo sapiens*, first appeared in that part of Africa occupied by Kenya. The explorative instinct of the human being made them start moving in that vast continent in what is described as the "out of Africa theory." As they were moving, so communities were also formed with every settlement they made. The first communities were therefore created.

Early Africans always knew there was a Supreme Being that was looking over all their activities and there had to be a way to communicate with him. One can, therefore, conclude that Black Africans started the first belief in a Supreme Being. However, both religions say that the first man created by God was Adam, from the earth, but his picture was shown to Africans as White, another deceit. In that case, then one can accept the claim by one southern African clergy that, since the earth is Black, it stands to reason that the first man created by God was also Black. Will White Christians accept that? I bet not, because to do so would portray them as liars and hypocrites.

I have put much emphasis on the Whiteman to mean the Western world, because the Blackman has suffered much in terms of humiliation at the hands of the West and its Christian culture. The Arabs, who were also under Western influence, could not do more than what they did as described above, also trading in Blacks, something that goes on to this date in Sudan and Mauritania. How can one explain the presence of blacks in Turkey, the famous black Russian poet and writer Alexander Pushkin, the presence of blacks of African ancestry in the Kingdom of Saudi Arabia? History has shown that the Whiteman is the most destructive being created by God. Examples include the conquistadores and the Aztec Indians of Mexico, the British and the Aborigines of Australia and Tasmania, and the Germans and what they did to the Hottentots of Namibia in the Black Holocaust doing the same to the Jews in the Holocaust.

When the Europeans brought the concept of Jesus Christ, they brought with it their way of life that the followers had to accept and follow; the Muslims did likewise. Colonialism has shown us that whatever religion the respective colonial power brought with it, there is always the accompanying culture or way of life. This leads to the belief that religion is part of culture.

According to Ralph Piddington, "Culture is the sum-total of the material and intellectual equipment whereby a people satisfy their biological and social needs and adapt themselves to their environment. Bronislaw Malinowski gave a broader definition of culture, which is "Culture is that complex whole, which includes knowledge, belief, art, law, morals, customs, and all other capabilities and habits acquired by man as a member of society." You can choose which definition you prefer.

After having accepted Christianity and/or Islam, what is now left of the Africans, apart from our color and our Negroid characteristics, to show that we are what we are—Black people—for most of the values we stand for now are tinted, either by European or Arabic influences? I agree that global interdependence is something that we must live with. But have the Japanese changed their culture for that of the West despite the deep interwoven economic and cultural ties between the two? Cannot the Blackman develop his own image and, at the same time, maintain whatever ties he wants with anybody? Does possession of a Mercedes Benz or a TV or a video make anyone of us a European or Japanese? *No!*

It is usually said that you can take a Blackman from his jungle, but you will never take that jungle out of him. That being true, then Blacks should hold on to the religion God prescribed for them before the Whiteman or the Arab came or before Blacks were sold into slavery. Nowhere did the Whiteman get it so easy as in Africa, where they launched a massive onslaught on the Blackman's belief system and all that he stands for. The Whiteman was in Asia but could not divert Asians from their religious beliefs, whether Buddhism, Hinduism, or Shintoism.

All the major churches in our societies have their parent bodies overseas, where material, intellectual, and religious support come to sustain the beliefs of Black people in these religions. There is also a limit in the hierarchy that does not allow a Blackman to get to the top. For the Anglican Church, this top position is claimed by the archbishop of Canterbury and for the Catholics, the Pope. Poverty, in Africa, has made Africans vulnerable and susceptible to all kinds of negative influences from outside.

For the Muslims, the only organized ones with schools in some African countries are the Ahmadis, a prosecuted sect in Pakistan whose leader resides in the United Kingdom. The Sunnis are all over Africa but not as missionaries, although they have schools where children are taught the Quran. The Muslims have no global leader like Christians have. And that, in my opinion, is responsible, in most of our societies, for the varied interpretations of the verses of the Quran.

Currently, young Islamic clerics from Western Europe, especially the United Kingdom and France, have started infiltrating Africa to compete again with Evangelical Christianity. Unlike the early Muslims who came as traders, these clerics have the backing of serious petrodollars to be able to entice especially young unemployed Africans. Again, Africans are sitting ducks, waiting for outsiders to trample upon them.

The part of the planet that God prescribed for Black people has been an area of political, commercial, and religious domination and exploitation. Now it has become a political, commercial, and religious dumping ground for outsiders. Religious bodies that are prosecuted in their countries of origin or have rather insignificant followership take their religions to the unsuspecting poor—the Black people of Africa. In December 1993, *The European* wrote, "The Protestant Church in Germany ... has seen attendance fall by more than 500,000 since 1991." In Africa, on the other hand, as poverty increases, churchgoing has rapidly increased, the opposite of what is happening in Europe. In the United Kingdom, very many churches have closed and been taken over by Muslims as the population of churchgoers has been dwindling over the years. Religion is losing its value to most members of the European and US populations as technology takes pride of place. Religion is no longer the opium of the people, as it has lost the mysticism it once commanded. In Africa where the population is the youngest in the world, there are no jobs for the youth, so they turn to religion, first preaching prosperity but now preaching miracles and fleecing the poor.

I have been wondering why it is necessary for anybody or any group of individuals to convince others to follow their religious beliefs. Somebody over his or her lifetime has established a connection with his or her Creator for everything. And then he or she is told or coaxed to abandon what he or she has believed for years. The American evangelical movement came into poor developing countries, exploiting the endemic poverty to cajole the people to join their ranks. There are great successes, mostly in Africa and South America. This has further divided the respective societies. The new churches have come with all that is necessary to maintain their followers—secondhand clothes, medication, food, and other needed supplies. But the question remains, why? These White evangelical preachers come from a country where Black people have been historically lynched and continue to be suppressed and randomly killed by White police, but they still want Black people to go along with them. Again, I ask the question. Why?

CHAPTER 8

The Advantages and Disadvantages of Foreign Religions in Africa

What benefits has the Blackman derived from these foreign religions?
Educational, Material, and Spiritual

Educational

T hose Black men who practiced Christianity were the first to get an education as we know it. And education was the exclusive domain of the colonial masters, whose religion was Christianity. That education brought with it jobs and salaries and their consequent privileges. This caused the "privileged" to assume a feeling of supremacy over the uneducated (or, rather, illiterate); alienation between the two ensued and, subsequently, discrimination took hold. Since the Muslims refused to send their children to school so that they would not become "unbelievers," they were the ones to feel the pinch. Becoming the least considered, they took up menial jobs—as watchmen, houseboys, messengers, and the like.

All this has led many Christians to erroneously equate Christianity with modernity. I say erroneously because the Jews, who are not Christians, cannot be described as uncivilized; neither can the Japanese and Chinese.

Could the Blackman have been educated without Christianity? What education did Islam bring to the Blackman?

Well, from all that can be derived from history and passed experiences, it was religious education that was offered by Islam. The Blackman was made to memorize the whole of the Quran, as there was no organized school whereby, he could learn Arabic. That education was confined only to the Quran. Thus, even the language was religious Arabic and not scientific so that, after the Quran, they enter the wicked world of reality to look for jobs that their religious education could not measure up to, so they reverted to where they were in their narrow world.

Industrial revolution and development took place in Christendom. That, I think, cannot be contested. Arabs adopted it, without changing their culture, although there were Christians in prominent jobs in some Arab governments, like Boutros Boutros-Ghali, former UN Secretary General from Egypt, and Tariq Aziz in late Saddam Hussein's government

What then is wrong with the Blackman? It is amazing, to see how black intellectuals struggle to justify their embrace of Western or Eastern culture through religion.

The result of the two educational processes is reflected on their respective followers. One feels superior to the other, and the other feels he is disregarded by the other. Thus, an unhealthy situation develops, and that continues to date. An example is Nigeria, where the Muslim north felt it must have more say in governance according to its geographical size. This reflects the truism in President Dr. Kwame Nkrumah's book *Class Struggle in Africa*, whereby African societies were divided into classes—the bourgeoisie and the peasants or illiterate ranks.

Material

Materially, again the Christians are the greatest beneficiaries. Christianity came in more organized groups as missionaries to preach the word of God to "heathens." Can you imagine trying to convert a people by calling them names? The converted enjoyed certain, or rather unlimited, privileges—housing, cars, allowances, and so on. So, when the colonial masters left, those whom they trained followed in their footsteps and enjoyed all these privileges, if not more—owning houses and cars and enjoying free international travel. These are the elites or les évolués in French. People who could otherwise have found it difficult to make ends meet with family commitments were suddenly able to do so.

Consequently, there has been an upsurge—a sort of vogue for young Black men to offer to preach the word of God, as doing so has become lucrative.

For the Muslims, at the start, there was no visible or marked material gains like there were with the Christians, as there were no organized groups or missionaries to emulate.

In later years, the Ahmadiyya movement came and established schools. They came as an organized community—in other words, as missionaries. But how many of my country men and women really knew they were a prosecuted sect in Pakistan under Zulfikar Ali Bhutto, president at the time? Their leader escaped to the United Kingdom, where he resided. The other Islamic sects did not recognize them as Muslims, but the people in Sierra Leone recognized them. Their schools had made important strides in education in Sierra Leone, and more and more of the students were contributing to the development of the nation.

After the Ahmaddis, the Iranians came. But apart from their Islamic sect, which had been strange or unknown to the Muslims in Sierra Leone, they also came strongly with politics. The Iranians quickly built a large mosque in the center of the capital, Freetown. Did the people know or were they aware that the Iranians were Shiites? That I cannot tell at the time of this writing, but it would further divide the people and make them easy targets for external domination.

As I indicated in my preface, Christianity can be associated with

Europeans and people of European descent, and Islam, with the Arabs and Arab-related people.

Just as there was an increase in Christian religious organizations, so did Islamic organizations expand—with huge, competitive sums of monies poured into both. This was, in fact, so much the case that Black men whose ancestors or heritage had nothing to do with either of the religions but who now stood to benefit immensely were prepared to do anything to defend their newfound privileges. Hence, the numerous and varied scandals that arose in these organizations.

Spiritual

Spiritually, one would be inclined to say that the Muslims benefited more, as they lost in both the educational and material categories. Most of the Muslims being preached to were basically illiterate, not only in English education but also in the religious Arabic education. As people who could not recheck what their Islamic preachers would tell them, they were left stagnant or, rather, deepening their ignorance. Most of our Muslim mothers have been victims of this, as most of what is typically preached is to put them in check.

Again, I will leave you to judge—did the Blackman gain spiritually from either of these religions?

Considering all that has been discussed, so far did our ancestors put up any resistance against the infiltration, domination, and eventual destruction of their ways of life and beliefs?

The history books, written by the British, say that Bai Bureh fought the British because of the hut tax imposed on his people. Was that all?

Bai Bureh was Sierra Leonean ruler and military strategist, who led the Temne and Loko uprising against British rule in 1898 when the British imposed the Hut Tax. He was a Muslim as well.

He tormented the British in a guerilla type warfare, acquiring the reputation for supernatural power and was believed to be bullet proof and to have the ability to become invisible or stay for long periods under water. The British put a bounty on his head without success.

He was however captured on November 11, 1898, then exiled to the

Gold Coast, present day Ghana. He was later brought back in 1905 and reinstated as Chief of Kasseh. He died in 1908.

Taking Bai Bureh for the powerful leader he was, could he have accepted the British way of life and belief in Christianity, being a Muslim, when he knew his power base could consequently be destroyed? One is inclined to disbelieve such a notion. Exiled to Ghana, his people were left at the mercy of the British, just like the mother baboon leaving its baby baboon in the hands of the hunter.

A combination of these factors led to the fight between Bai Bureh and the British, and when he was defeated, those Christians who were enjoying the privileges that their religion gave them made songs in mockery of him. Christians were killed because, I feel, they were seen and understood to be protectors of the Whiteman's culture.

Some people tell me that the first White missionaries who went to Taiama, a town in Sierra Leone on the highway to Bo City in the South, the McGgregors, were killed and their bodies buried by the old bridge. Other stories tell of how some other White missionaries were relegated to driving birds in rice farms in the Bumpeh area and so on, again during the Hut Tax War.

How did Black men (our ancestors) understand or interpret the creation of the universe without reference to the Bible or the Quran? If Black men lived in organized societies at the time the Bible or the Quran was written and the Blackman believed and still believes in a Supreme Being and was praying to him, then the Blackman had his own interpretation or understanding of the universe and the world around him.

From research I have made, the following come out: In traditional African beliefs, the forces of creation and the things created are part of the same reality. But Christianity and Islam brought a God who was or is separate from the created, enthroned in heaven while humans have been made rulers over the animals below. The natural world was, thus, made a servant of humans, rather than a partner.

CHAPTER 9

Post-independence Africa

The most glaring dilemma for the Africans was how to govern themselves. The effect of all the different influences on the African started showing. As Dr. Kwame Nkrumah wrote in *Class Struggle in Africa*, Africans were already divided, not only by tribe and foreign religions, but also by class, which categorized the populations by economic and political class. This has been the curse of Africa to date.

During colonialism, the individual colonial power subjected its African populations to its respective governance system. For the British, it was indirect rule. This was shown in an exchange between Sir Ernest Beoku-Betts and the British government in 1918. Beoku-Betts asked whether "the color of a man's skin is to make any difference within the Empire" and called for "equality of the races." The British government, through the Ormsby-Gore pronouncement of 1916, restated its position that, "The English man has naturally an instinctive dislike of 'assimilation'. We like to keep our life distinct from that of other races European or not. The more another people acquire our culture, our outlook, and social habits; very often the wider becomes the gulf between us ... We frequently get on better with people different from us, and we appreciate the differences more than the points we have in common" (Professor Akintola Wyse, *The Krio of Sierra Leone: An Interpretive History*). This was British arrogance being expressed when the empire was booming.

On the contrary, the French came up with the ideology of

"assimilation," in which the Africans in the respective territories would be accepted as French by adopting French culture and language. Those who did were given privileges—to show the others that they would benefit by joining them. The respective African leaders were then accepted into the French parliament, in contrast to the British. Through that policy, the French exerted total control over the territories, so much so that, at independence, the respective African leaders were forced to acquiesce to all the demands of the French—like surrendering about 80 percent of the annual revenue to the Bank of France in perpetuity. This policy has impoverished most if not all the former French territories, and as estimates go, costs them billions of dollars annually. Now, the information is out and the whole of Africa is waiting to see how the French settles that.

The class struggle in Africa has made it much easier for the former colonial powers to incite and manipulate military coups right across the continent—in Ghana, Nigeria, Sierra Leone, Liberia, and others. The French never let go its former territories as leader after leader was removed by force or physically eliminated. And in other parts of the continent, it has encouraged internecine wars, mostly tribal. French intervention in post-independence Africa is whole political science study on its own, better left for others to write about.

The continent has seen the domination of White minority governments in former Rhodesia, now Zambia and Zimbabwe; Namibia; and South Africa. In other cases, Africans had to revolt against colonial and White rule. This happened in Kenya with the Mau Mau Uprising, Mozambique with FRELIMO, South Africa with the ANC, Angola with the MPLA, and Namibia with SWAPO. All these wars were fueled by the cold war between the United States of America and the then USSR, especially in Mozambique, Angola, and Guinea Bissau.

One interesting aspect about the case of Mozambique stemmed from the indoctrination of Africans and the use of the Bible to tell them to turn the other cheek when given a slap on one. When FREMILO fired the first shot, and the rank-and-file soldier saw a white man fall dead for the first time, that erased all the myth embedded in them that white people never died as they were taken out of the country at the point of death. That emboldened the rank-and-file fighters, ensuring them that they were doing the right thing to liberate their country.

One other interesting factor worth highlighting was that Black Africans, who were used to being bossed around - by some assessments by low-ranking white men, gradually saw how frightened these very people were at the sight of death. Some were saved by the very Africans they felt so empowered over. Seeing this, erased the fear and respect the Africans had for their "masters." Returning home, the equation started changing and transformation took root. Colonial powers were already weakened militarily after WWII. Rather than holding on to the territories with force, the European powers agreed to decolonize the continent.

Politically, Africans became divided between the educated and enlightened and the peasants or uneducated. The division also went into tribal affiliations, as party politics was becoming a particularly important part of life in postcolonial Africa.

Africa's defenses and economies were in the kindergarten stage and very friable and vulnerable to machinations and bullying by their respective colonial powers, Britain, France, and Portugal being the major culprits. Exploitation, which was the main reason for invading and subduing Africa in the first place, was going on unabated. Anywhere there was resistance to any colonial power, it was crushed. The typical example was in the Congo, which was the greatest exporter of uranium needed and used by powers like the United States, Britain, and France. When Congo was given its independence from Belgium, a new leader emerged, Patrice Lumumba, who resisted the powers. He was killed, and his own countryman, Joseph Desire Mobutu, later Mobutu Sese Seku, was used to perform the act, thereby intimidating any other Congolese who might think of copying him.

Similar policies were adopted in Guinea Conakry when Sekou Toure said a definite *non* to President Charles De Gaulle of France. His reply was, "Mesdames et messieurs, nous n'avons plus rien a faire ici" (We have nothing more to do here). As a result, they removed everything physically French, even the electric cables. That intimidated the rest of French West Africa, driving home the price of resisting. And it softened the way for France to get virtually all its colonies, as has been recently revealed, to acquiesce to all French demands. Those demands included the colonies surrendering almost 80 percent of their budgets to the

French treasury in perpetuity, giving the French the right to intervene anytime French interests were threatened, and purchasing exclusively from France. This was all in line with what former French President Jacques Rene Chirac said: "We bled Africa for four and a half centuries. We looted their raw materials, then we told them lies that the Africans are good for nothing. In the name of religion, we destroyed their culture. And after being rich at their expense, we now steal their brains through miseducation and propaganda to prevent them from enacting Black retribution against us."

These colonial arrangements were brought to the public's knowledge by the former ambassador for the AU (African Union) to the United States of America, Ambassador Dr. Arikana Chihombori-Quao. The revelation very much embarrassed the French, and she had to leave her post as a result.

Dr. Arikana Chihombori-Quao has been giving speeches in US institutions over the years. In one of those speeches at a Historical Black College on the topic of Time for Africa, she said this:

> What color is the devil, I pause for two seconds; most of you would say black.
>
> What color are the angels? Let me guess again, most of you would say white.
>
> Who has seen either? And yet we accept it. So, you take a group of people, you say the color black is associated with the devil. Everything black is bad, you wear black to go to funerals, the villains in movies are black, everything undesirable is black. You take a group of people, and say you too are black. No matter how we try, as black mothers, to raise our children at home and tell them they are black and beautiful, the minute they step foot outside that door, they are immersed in nothing but negativity about that which they represent. How do you raise a child with good self-esteem in such a world?
>
> Then I took it back a step further. Growing up in my village in Zimbabwe, the British did not come to Zimbabwe until 1896.

Prior to that, we had our own Gods that we worshipped with spirit mediums, which were intermediaries to the higher power. They had no color until the British arrived. Then the British began to, remember the missionaries were sent to Africa to teach us how to read but not how to reason. So, we were programmed to receive that which they wanted us to receive. So, one of the things they taught us was the issue of black and white. Remember in 1896, in my country we did not have those colors. I was not referred to as black, I was African. But somehow, we were just told that you were black, the other race white. Then the other race you take white color. You say white is pure, the angels are white, you put on white to go to weddings, white for christening, then you take another group of people and tell them they are white. So, the children are raised that they are beautiful, everything that they represent is perfect and they step outside the door, the world validates what they have been told at home.

Now, you take these two children, one is surrounded by nothing but negativity about that which they represent. The other is surrounded by nothing but positivity about that which they represent. How do you expect those children to look at themselves as equals?

These are some of the subliminal messages that are being passed on to our children, and in my own assessment, when you look at it from the African point of view, it explains why some of our leaders, people who are supposed to represent us when they sit across the table with others who do not look like them, they automatically feel inferior. It is a serious problem. It affects our ability to feed our children as mothers, affects our ability to provide for our children to go to school, provide good healthcare systems, provide good infrastructure. It starts right there. The failure to stand up and defend that which you believe in and defend that which is blatantly wrong.

The British MI6 and the American CIA were forever present and hands-on in forcing Africans to go along or be removed from power.

The colonial powers were in control of the economies of their respective colonies and knew their weaknesses and strengths. After the Second World War, the victorious Western powers, under the tutelage of the United States, created financial organizations, IMF, and the World Bank, meant to regulate and control the world economies. African countries were basically exporters of raw materials, whereas their former colonial powers were fixing the prices of their commodities. This has been used to control or destroy Africa's economies.

As Dr. Chihombori-Quao said, the effect of colonial indoctrination becomes glaring each time an educated African comes across somebody who is White with the same educational level as him or her, the inferiority complex kicks in immediately. The result of the encounter between these two counterparts will always show how the Black African has been acquiescent to the interlocutor.

Immediately after independence, those who were among the elite— the Anglophone and les évolués in Francophone Africa—were the ones who suddenly found themselves face-to-face with their former bosses, making them feel elevated in stature but innately feeling inferior. Suddenly, they saw themselves sleeping in hotels they would never have dreamed about, eating in posh restaurants, and enjoying the amenities their former bosses enjoyed—all of which made them accept everything from their former bosses. The fact that they were there to fight for their peoples took second and third places. These are the very people who became superbly intolerant of dissenting voices and were always ready to harm their opponents to maintain their privileged positions.

For the Whiteman, former colonialist, dealing with an African leader who was corrupt worked well. They had, after all, created the very privileges these leaders enjoyed. Mobutu Sese Seku comes to mind immediately, as he was put in charge of the Congo Republic, later Zaire and now Democratic Republic of the Congo. During his time, he prosecuted and chased anybody who spoke against him, thus becoming the absolute ruler of the vast land in the heart of Africa.

Étienne Tshisekedi, one-time minister of Foreign Affairs for Mobutu, in his book "*Mobutu et L'Incarnation du Mal Zairois*" described in detail how, on a regular basis, minerals from mines in the country were taken by plane loads, with the proceeds deposited in Swiss Banks. This siphoning goes on to date, as again reiterated by Dr. Chihombori-Quao, who said that flying over the DRC, large runways could be seen from which only exceptionally large planes can land and take off. Precious minerals very much needed for present-day technology are, for the most part, only found in the DRC. Hence, multinational corporations are active in the politics of the country, bribing the local leaders. Mobutu was just one of a large cabal of corrupt African leaders, who behaved as if they were all born of the same parents, depositing money abroad since independence in varying degrees.

This inferiority complex and the eagerness to be like the Whiteman, has dominated each encounter the post-independent African has had with the Whiteman, except in sports. This is not an academic conclusion, but an opinion based on things I experienced growing up, going abroad to further my education, and returning to Africa. I cannot give any statistical figures, and I know some may want to challenge me. Living in any African society, it is easy to see and feel what I am talking about.

When a Whiteman goes to Africa and into the very interior of any country, he is never harassed. People are always ready to receive him with welcoming arms and help him get what he went for. Let us contrast that with the reception any black man gets in a white neighborhood where he/she is stopped and frisked and humiliated or the black African soccer players get in Europe while they are playing and entertaining white spectators. They are called "monkeys" with bananas thrown at them on the pitches. Despite all that humiliation, black African soccer players still go to Europe. Why? Is it to teach white people out of racism, an impossible task or plain and simple, poverty?

The concept of White people forever comparing Black people to monkeys to me is intriguing—especially given and despite all the centuries White men spent exploiting Africa and having sex and children with Black women. How is this the case? How have Africans in the continent reacted? Why have they not reacted in like manner to the White people, who continually go to Africa to exploit the continent? The only explanation I can come to is one of a feeling of inferiority complex. I really hope I am wrong and that there is a more tangible and understandable explanation.

Most Africans, who now come into discussions with White people representing their countries, are well educated. But why do we have the same reaction of inferiority complex?

Since my emphasis is on the African continent, let me go back to what I wrote earlier, citing the late Dr. Kwame Nkrumah's *Class Struggle in Africa*. Nkrumah ascribed that struggle to colonialism and, I dare add, also Christianity, which the colonialists used very well to their advantage. He spoke about the bourgeoisie and the peasants. Christianity was the fuel used to create such divisions, as those who were converted to or accepted Christianity were educated and served as the corps of the civil service. These were the people who took over after the colonial masters left and assumed and demanded the same respect given to their masters. They accepted and propagated European values through Christianity and defended those values vehemently, as they had to show how civilized they were. They looked at the non-Christians, mainly Muslims and the peasantry, as not modern.

With time, the children of the peasantry, mainly Muslims, also became educated. Some saw the benefits of becoming Christians, mainly Catholics, and got the education their parents could not have. I saw the picture of a Catholic bishop, who took his mother, a Muslim, to Ramadan prayers while he waited in his car. Unfortunately, that group of Africans also gravitated to the mentality of a superiority complex over those left behind.

Some of these educated Africans, for the most part in West Africa, found themselves in international organizations, making decisions that affected the very people they were expected to protect and defend. They could not, as they had to agree with the missions of the organizations before getting the jobs.

These were the ones who now constituted the most serious problems for the African peoples. They become the bridge or liaison between the Western financial institutions and the African governments. They were ready to dismiss any arguments or criticisms of these institutions, on the grounds that they always knew better than the locals. But when given jobs to help develop their countries, they faltered, because they had been used to being supervised.

During the presidency of Siaka Stevens in Sierra Leone, he was heavily criticized for having majority of half-baked and even illiterate ministers of cabinet. He then decided to bring into his cabinet many of his fellow citizens with PhDs. This group of highly educated Africans glorified open corruption. What went wrong? Many educated Africans believe first and foremost that their education has placed them beyond rebuke—that they are leadership material and are free to do whatever they like. This attitude is always displayed in professions like medicine, law, engineering, architecture, and the like. It was because of the misbehavior of these PhDs that Siaka Stevens made a pronouncement that eventually destroyed the moral and educational fabric that had prevailed in the country: "They say Bailor Barrie, you say Davidson Nicol." Bailor Barrie was an extraordinarily rich businessman, and Dr. Davidson Nicol was an academic and principal of Fourah Bay College, the early renowned university in Sierra Leone. It was interpreted differently by different people, but what was clear was that a generation or two of young Sierra Leoneans believed him and abandoned schooling. Interest in education plummeted.

CHAPTER 10

Removing the Interruption of the Intellectual Chain

A fricans have been mocked internationally for having sit-tight presidents for life. After all my years living in Africa, my understanding is that they took the place of the colonial masters and dared anyone challenge them. And with the Cold War active during those years, they were able to play one power against another—Mobutu of Congo, Hastings Banda of Malawi, Dos Santos of Angola, Paul Biya of Cameroon, and a few others. With the collapse of the USSR, global politics and international relations suddenly changed. The West demanded multiparty democracy with free and fair elections. In quick succession, these sit-tight leaders started falling. Mobutu was removed from power, fell ill, and later died. Hastings Banda was forced to accept multiparty democracy, and he lost power and died in South Africa.

There were those leaders who were removed because of their opposition to continued Western domination of African affairs. The first and most notable was Dr. Kwame Nkrumah, who was removed through a coup orchestrated by the American CIA; all his development programs were reversed, holding Ghana back years in development. He was replaced by a leader very much in the playbook of the West as an example to the rest of the leaders to play it by the West's rules or be removed from power.

Since independence, there has been no deliberate effort by any of the leaders to reprogram the African peoples—to free them from the mentality of serfdom and inferiority complex to the Whiteman. That has been difficult because of the entrenchment of Christianity and Islam in the psyche of the African people. Dr. Kwame Nkrumah never wrote about the influence of these religions in the minds of his people, as he also took it for granted, and there was no reason to raise it.

Today, the African intellectual, when cornered about his or her allegiance to these religions, always counters, rather helplessly, that it is a matter of faith. At first, I thought they were just using it as an escape from their gullibility. But, in fact, their reaction can be viewed this way—that to capture a baby baboon, the mother must be killed to detach the baby from its natural survival. Through this killing, the baby baboon is left at the mercy and machination of the human being responsible, thereby causing the baby to lose contact with all that should make him a baboon. This can be seen with zoo animals and those kept as domestic pets. Most of these animals die when and if taken back to their natural environments.

For the human beings that we all are, the situation is completely different, as we have intellect and the power of adaptability, meaning that the Africans were able to adapt to the new situation they were subjected to for their own survival and benefit. So, they accepted the new religions and, in most cases, tried to adapt the new religions to their own needs. Examples include the Adejobi's Church of the Lord (Aladura) in West Africa, the Church of Simon Kimbangu in the Congo, and the many different churches given tribal names to attract only people of a certain tribe. The Muslims also, especially in Sierra Leone, named their mosques after their respective tribes. These eventually became the first point of contact when they arrived in a big city, searching for their kith and kin.

The adaptation has reached such a level that the line of demarcation between these religions and the African beliefs can hardly be seen.

This, in my view, is an interruption in the intellectual chain of the Blackman. And until and except a reprograming takes place, the Blackman will always feel and be treated as inferior to the Whiteman.

For those who were not born in Africa, please understand that my awakening came about when I lived and worked in Sierra Leone in West Africa and my whole perspective has been based on what I saw and experienced there when growing up.

There are Black people who have lived for centuries in different parts of the world—mother Africa, the Americas, North, Central, and South, Europe, the Arabian Peninsula, and India.

The most vociferous and vibrant Blacks are those in the United States of America, Europe, and Africa.

In Africa, the independence movements brought the affairs of black Africans to world attention. The liberation wars in Algeria, Rhodesia, Kenya, Namibia, Angola, Guinea Bissau, Mozambique, and South Africa, all brought to light the brutality of European colonial rule in Africa.

In the 60s, the Civil Rights Movement in the US brought to world's attention how blacks in the US were being brutalized and marginalized. The US press was an inadvertent companion in making the world know what blacks were suffering at the hands of the white majority.

For those Blacks in Central and South America, there has been a dearth of news about their lives that could have ignited the similar reactions as with blacks in other areas. Some Africans in my age group, started knowing and seeing blacks in Central and South America, when FIFA World Cup football started going worldwide.

One major factor, I think, for the dearth of news from those areas is language, unlike the Caribbean Islands, which are basically English speaking. English language being more international than Spanish and Portuguese, makes it much easier to disseminate news from those areas. Is it the possibility that prominent individuals among the black populations in Central and South America, are quickly eliminated to keep them quiet? Research must be done in that sphere.

When I checked Google to further educate myself, I found this: "In Latin America's colonial period, about 15 times as many African slaves were taken to Spanish and Portuguese colonies than to the U.S. Today, about 130 million people of African descent live in Latin America, making up roughly a quarter of the total population, according to estimates from the "Project on Ethnicity."

I just wonder why not as much has been heard about them as has been heard about their kith and kin in the United States. Brazil has the largest population of Blacks transported to the Americas as slaves, about ninety-one million people. Blacks in the United States, as well as in the rest of the Americas, have mostly excelled in sports, especially soccer in Central and South America, boxing, track-and-field, baseball, basketball, and American football in the United States. Blacks have also taken part in politics and are represented in the US Congress even up to the presidency, as Barack Hussein Obama became the 44th President of the USA.

Black innovations in the US have been pushed under the rug for far too long but thanks to education, more and more of those stories and coming out to light. The movie "The Hidden Figures" narrated how three black women scientists, Katherine Johnson, Dorothy Vaughan, and Mary Jackson, helped the US succeed in space exploration. Their stories would stay hidden until it was no more. It can be safely said that Blacks in the United States have succeeded, for the most part, better than their kith and kin elsewhere in the Americas as their stories have been told. Thanks to the internet with the powerful search engines like Google, Yahoo and others and social media in general, the stories of black innovations can no longer be hidden as had been done hitherto. Reactions to blacks have unfortunately been upgraded to maintain white superior feeling over the rest of mankind, especially black people.

Having said all that, I urge every Black person of African ancestry to find out why there are no Blacks in Argentina. The story is chilling, and it further convinces me that Black people everywhere, must be reprogrammed to face the ills White people have been ready to unleash on them, as nothing that glitters is gold.

Despite all the gains that can be hailed, Black people in the United States have, for centuries, been struggling, fighting against the wickedness of the Whiteman who went around the world preaching the word of Jesus Christ to love thy neighbor as thyself. The late Rev. Dr. Martin Luther King Jr said that "in America, the most segregated time is 11am on Sunday" when whites go exclusively to their churches and blacks do likewise. Blacks move into white neighborhoods and whites move out. That is indeed love thy neighbor as thy self. Blacks are driven out whole, out of neighborhoods through gentrification – Harlem and parts of Washington DC. Black people have been brutalized and killed by these people just for telling them to obey their own Constitution, written without them in mind.

Why were Blacks in the US, not roundly exterminated, as was done in Argentina as so vividly described by various sources upon a simple Google search? In the United States, I believe because blacks were commodity. To exterminate them would mean loss of revenue and prestige. In the Americas, when slavery ended, the slaves were simply left on their own with no protection whatsoever except from God.

The Eugenic movement came and a whole lot of horrible and unspeakable things were done to blacks that, some say, were copied by Hitler in exterminating the Jews in the Holocaust. Notable black people, like Dr. Martin Luther King Jr., Malcolm X, and Medgar Evers, were all killed while fighting for recognition for Blacks at all levels of society. Young Black men have long been murdered by police, and now even young Black women are no longer spared. The prison industrial concept was brought about to take the place of slavery, imprisoning young able-bodied Black men at the slightest infringement for the maximum number of years and depriving them later of their rights to vote. They are then used to work for pittances as salaries.

What about Europe, which had been the vehicle for transporting Black people as slaves to different parts of the American continent? Similar attitudes have been expressed to Black people, although on a much lower scale. Police brutality has been the common denominator, with inherent protection given to the police by the State. Poor housing, low-paid jobs, and restricted access to good health facilities for Blacks are just as prevalent as in the United States. It is as if centuries of interaction and exploitation of the continent meant nothing to Black African peoples. The French—who have continued to enjoy the better part of the exploitation, with former colonies giving up 80 percent of their annual budgets—still have not given Black people in their midst the respect and protection needed. Black Africans are still being ridiculed and medically experimented on.

In 2013 the Black Lives Matter movement, was formed after the acquittal of a white Latino man, George Zimmerman for the reckless, and brutal killing of a young black man, Trayvon Martin 2012. Here we are again May 25, 2020, another young black man, George Floyd 46, was seen on TV the world over with the knee of a white Minneapolis police officer pressing on his neck while handcuffed and on the ground until he died. This thus brought out into the open all the lies the police have been saying when they encounter blacks where there are no witnesses. The lies inherent in their religion vis-à-vis Black people and all the wicked things done to Black people for so long have been exposed. There is a demand for history written by Whites about Blacks to be revisited. Statues of famous slave traders have been brought down, along with that of the most notorious Whiteman in history, King Leopold II of Belgium. He was also known as the Butcher of the Congo, for the killing over ten million Black people in the Congo. His statue was brought down in Antwerp, Belgium. They talk of Hitler exterminating six million Jews. What about King Leopold II, who killed ten million Black people, old and young, with no consideration of gender? Does it mean that the killing of six million Jews is of less historical importance than the killing of ten million Black Africans? I am not downplaying the Holocaust. But extermination is extermination; in both cases, people, human beings, whether they be White or Black, were being exterminated. Let White people be fair, for they are not the only humans on this earth.

Since biblical times, human beings have been moving from place to place looking for something good for their existence. Gunpowder was eventually discovered through interaction with Chinese people by the British, who saw its importance in combating and overpowering their enemies in the battlefields. This helped the British to go around the world subduing vulnerable people, thereby becoming the most important nation of its time in the world. Hence, the British Empire, the East India Company—Britannia ruled the oceans.

Did the British and other European people have visas to go exploit other parts of the world? No. But they did it anyway and built up their nations physically and mentally, thus developing what we see in the world today, called white supremacy. The British have had influence in every world idea since slavery to the 1980s and 1990s, when their power started waning with membership of the European Union.

The policies of colonialism, with its exploitation of third world countries and peoples, have so much impoverished these nations that the process of osmosis has started, and these very European countries are shouting holy hell. Just like in biblical times, so it is nowadays; people are moving around looking for greener pastures.

When the European colonial powers gave independence to their territories, a new realization developed. The near free acquisition of raw materials from the territories was dwindling down and the threat Germany posed was not to be overlooked and had to be put under check. The European Economic Community was then created through the Treaty of Rome in 1957 for the signature countries to trade freely among them while watching the Germans. Britain was not an initial signatory. Britain made two other attempts at membership but was blocked by French President Charles De Gaulle, who feared, as some of learned, the influence or leverage of the US through Britain. Britain was finally accepted in 1973 after the end of De Gaulle's term.

As a result, Britain began reducing its engagement with the Commonwealth countries that were formed after independence. Immigration from those countries was reduced as Britain was getting fully engaged with the EU. The other countries of the EU did the same as Britain. France, which had extensive relationships with her former colonies, tightened immigration. Holland and Italy all followed suit thereby creating Fortress Europe. Even the United States of America, which is the land of immigrants, also started heavily scrutinizing the influx of immigrants that came to a crescendo when Donald Trump became President of the USA.

The refugee crisis that began because of the ISIS occupation of Iraq and Northern Syria, was so massive that it jolted European nations from their slumber to outright fear and animosity. Human beings made it seem easy to go through national borders that right wing politicians took advantage of and started preaching nationalism. Victor Orban, Prime Minister of Hungary, used the refugee crisis very much to his own advantage and closed the borders of Hungary to all non-Hungarians seeking refuge. He eventually tightened his grip on power using undemocratic policies have brought a clash with EU values of free movement of peoples.

During these difficult times, Angela Merkel, Chancellor of Germany, saw the need to open the doors of her country to about a million refugees with the hope of reviving the aging workforce of Germany. The policy backfired as many Germans feared the Islamization that would follow, Germany being a Christian state. Her popularity plummeted and that has led to her rethinking her continued place in German politics. In October 2018, Angela Merkel announced she was no longer going to contest for the leadership of her party, the CDU, come 2021, which would have been her fifth term.

After collapse of the then USSR and the fall of the Berlin wall, the EU decided to open membership to former Warsaw Pact countries which were under the grip of the then, Soviet Union. This brought in a flood of immigrants from Eastern Europe especially to the island of Britain, much to the consternation of the British. A political crisis ensued that eventually led to the referendum dubbed Brexit 23 June 2016, the exit of Britain from the EU. The British decided to quit the EU. Losing all the gains that were inherent in EU membership, the British have resorted to rebuilding the Commonwealth.

The death of George Floyd brought the Black Lives Matter movement into even more prominence, as more people both in the United States and in Europe and, indeed, the world over came to the realization of what the movement had been preaching about the treatment Black people, especially young Black men, and women, were getting at the hands of mainly White police officers.

Adom Getachew, in his article in *The New York Times* of July 27, 2020, wrote:

> Now, partly riding the global surge of Black Lives Matter mobilizations, calls for decolonization have swept Europe's former imperial metropoles. In Bristol, England, last month, protesters tore down the statue of Edward Colston, the director of the Royal African Company, which dominated the African slave trade in the 17th and 18th centuries. Across Belgium, protesters have focused on statues of King Leopold II, who ruled the Congo Free State (now the Democratic Republic

of Congo) as his personal property from 1885 to 1908. King Phillipe II of Belgium recently expressed "regret" for his ancestor's brutal regime, which caused the death of 10 million people."

He wrote further that, "By tearing down or defacing these statues, protesters burst open the national narrative and force a confrontation with the history of empire. This is a decolonization of the sensory world, the illusion that empire was somewhere else."

For centuries, both Christianity and Islam have been competing for the hearts and minds of Africans, but both are quiet about Black Lives Matter. In the United States, most White evangelicals are opposed to the movement, some even describing it as a terrorist movement, refusing to take into consideration the rampant brutality and killing of young blacks for no other reason than they are black. There is a serious and willful misunderstanding within the hierarchy of the Catholic Church in the United States about the BLM. For me, this is serious as the US church has an important leverage in the Church. The Catholic family in the continent of Africa, home of black people, is huge. Are Catholics in Europe and the US going to tell their fellow members in Africa that the BLM is evil or is a terrorist movement? I urge caution as the Church has been making these mistakes misunderstanding people especially from third world environments. I am old enough to remember the Church's stance on family planning which was and still is the idea of Dr Henry Kissinger meant to control third world populations especially in Africa, so that the West can freely exploit the earthly minerals; the Liberation theology of Latin American priests made the priests mouthpieces for the problems of their parishioners. They were banned by the Vatican not to talk about or 'meddle' in local politics. In the Republic of Ireland, a referendum had to be conducted to finally decide on abortion. The Church lost in all these cases as the realities prevailed.

I hope that white people and their institutions will finally realize that black people are not ignorant and with social media, news that could have taken years to reach us now takes nanoseconds. The BLM is not a terrorist movement just as the Civil Rights Movement of the sixties was not Communist. The unfortunate part of the story is that most Christians and Muslims in Africa know nothing about what these religions think about Black people in their countries of origin—Europe and the United States.

What are Africans in the continent going to do about reactions to the BLM? Are they just not going to pay attention but continue the faith? Or are they going to reflect and search their consciences as to what continued adherence to these religions, which have little or no regard for Black lives, means?

This has been the view of most educated and enlightened Black Africans who adhere to these religions—faith, not what the religions do, evil or not.

The psyche of Black Africans has been so dominated by these two religions that the same length of time used to indoctrinate and brainwash them will be necessary to do the reverse.

In my humble and singular way, I have tried to contribute to the African solution in a way my predecessors never did. They, apparently, found it difficult to draw the line of demarcation between what our ancestors believed in and what was brought to them but, instead, blended both to come to an acceptable situation. They dealt with political and economic aspects of European and Arab domination, failing to see the negative effects all that had on the psyche of Africans, putting us in the difficult situation we are in today.

I believe in God, the Creator of the universe, like my ancestors. But I am aware and awake to the negative effect of these two religions on my fellow Africans. And I detest it. There is no one religion that can lead the human being to God, as nobody has been able to see him. Africans have been deceived into accepting everything said by the preachers of these religions, primarily to dominate and exploit us, as clearly codified in King Leopold II's letter to his missionaries. Any African reading that letter, which I reproduced whole, must be awake to the truth of European and Arab domination of our people, mainly for economic reasons. To the present day, they both continue to treat Black people not as equal creations of God but as sub-humans to be maltreated at will. To the amazement of whites and Arabs, who forced this lie on them, Africans by their reaction, have accepted the description given to them—that they are inferior beings with inferior intellect. African intellectuals are also heavily complicit in all this propaganda making African people believe it is their fault that they are poor. These intellectuals are given privileges to work in Western Financial Institutions with salaries that extremely far exceed what their native countries can give them. They later become mouthpieces to convince African leaders in making their people poor. Once that takes effect, these leaders can then agree to any conditionalities given to them for loans. Am I saying that African leaders are not guilty through bad governance? No. In Sierra Leone in the 80s, the president wanted to host the OAU annual leaders conference even against all expert advice including that of the then Governor of the National Bank, Sam Bangura, and the Bank of England as it was a guarantor for the Bank of Sierra Leone then. Some have accused Siaka Stevens of the brutal killing later of the bank governor. Again, the national railway was dismantled on advice from the IMF with some prominent people then in government being accused of complicity. All these actions stem from the fact that Siaka Stevens was greedy and wanted power at all costs, especially the description of Chairman of the OAU, which he took as his greatest achievement in the context of continental power; also inherent in all this, inferiority complex as the advice was from white specialists. These actions sent Sierra Leone backwards and has never recovered economically or otherwise, since the 80s as the national reserves were emptied. Similar actions have been taken by African leaders over the years since independence. To escape any criticisms, it became fashionable for them to blame the West. But former President Ibrahim Babangida of Nigeria disagreed with that, saying once that 'it is high time African leaders stop blaming the West for everything bad that occurs in Africa". That struck a chord in the minds of many Africans at the time, provoking an introspection into governance, in general, in the continent.

For Africans to come out of this predicament, a total reprogramming of the African psyche must be undertaken; the history books have to be rewritten with a very heavy slant to the African perspective, civics education, control or eradication of corruption a tall order, programs meant to indoctrinate the people about themselves like it happened in Ethiopia with 'Ethiopia first', and in Europe where, for centuries, young whites have been indoctrinated to believe that they are superior to blacks irrespective of the level of education of those blacks, job opportunities to reduce the dependence of young Africans on miracles rather than innovation.

Let me just give a shout out to President Paul Kagame of Rwanda. He, in my assessment, has been the singular leader who has made it a national policy to begin to reprogram the way his people think and behave. I want to say here without delving into the Civil War, that when Paul Kagame came to power after the genocide that killed up to if not over a million people, calm and trust needed to be established for the people to have faith in whatever the government was bringing.

The judicial system had to be such that the people would accept it. Western style of jurisprudence was anathema to majority of Rwandans and indeed black Africans. The judicial systems left behind by the colonialists all over Africa have been so fraught with bad governance as the indigenous people have no faith in it and those, whose task it is, to educate the people and make them understand the system, refuse to do so rather taking advantage of the people's ignorance to their own advantage, especially in politics.

The Gacaca courts were established. These were a blend of local conflict-resolution traditions with modern punitive legal system. In the words of President Kagame this was an "African solution to African problems." The courts have been useful in maintaining peace and tranquility needed so much at the time and henceforth. Was it a 100% full proof? I do not think so as people complained a lot expressing their dissatisfaction on certain issues as regards others. But that is democracy. A government cannot satisfy all the people all the time.

So many conflicts among the black peoples of Africa are settled by "native law and custom" not the European way. African leaders only needed to call on our own historians to research those aspects of our history, how our ancestors governed their populations and to try to modernize those methods or systems. It is said that for the TIV tribe in Nigeria, the elders will assemble under a tree with shade and discuss and discuss until a consensus is arrived at. President Paul Kagame continues to reprogram his people, albeit with some success. The only fear is, after him, will the policy continue like it is in Singapore after Lee Kuan Yew, who developed Singapore into a top global financial hub? Osagyefo Dr

Kwame Nkrumah, former President of Ghana, started a system but was removed from power by the West and all his policies thrown away setting Ghana back for decades.

If, by any miracle, African leaders can be convinced about the picture I have presented, then a lot will begin to be made to remove that interruption in the intellectual chain of the black man and to allow him to think properly.

Oh! What a dilemma.

CONCLUSION

I am also not oblivious to the fact that you may be inclined to reject my ideas outright because

1. probably, they are coming from a Blackman and not worthy of your attention,
2. your religion may have created such "sophistication" in your mind that the ideas presented here provoke a memory of the "backwardness" you may not want to be reminded of,
3. your religion may have caused such mysticism and fanaticism in you that such ideas can only be described as blasphemous and not worth associating with, or
4. you are at peace with your beliefs and do not want to be bothered.

I accept whichever case applies to you but will still urge you, all the same, to read this book again and again and again. It will finally dawn on you that your religion is not under question but that the Blackman's image has been so battered in history that it is high time that image is revealed in its rightful perspective.

It was the late Jamaican reggae singer Peter Tosh who sang that "Wherever you come from, as long as you are a Blackman, you're an African." You might not have been born in Mother Africa because of slavery, but you are indeed an African.

Black people have mounted any amount of resistance throughout the history of humankind, since the first encounter between Black and White people, and that continues to date. The Black Lives Matter movement is the most recent iteration of that resistance or struggle. It has caused a serious reawakening to revisit colonial history and the way

Black people have been and are being brutalized in the United States, Europe and indeed the rest of the world, especially China.

Irrespective of your status in society, your level of sophistication, your affluence, or whatever else, you are and will always remain Black.

Do not ever forget that.

Once more, I thank you.

Printed in the United States
By Bookmasters